D0379963

GARDENING AMONG FRIENDS

~

65 Practical Essays by
Master Gardeners

GARDENING AMONG FRIENDS

~

65 Practical Essays by
Master Gardeners

~

EDITED BY
BARBARA J. EUSER

SOLAS HOUSE
PALO ALTO

Copyright © 2006 Barbara J. Euser. All rights reserved.

For permission to reprint essays in this volume, grateful acknowledgment is made to the holders of copyright whose names appear on pages 212-218.

Solas House is an imprint of Travelers' Tales. Solas House and Travelers' Tales are trademarks of Travelers' Tales, Inc., 853 Alma Street, Palo Alto, California, 94301. www.travelerstales.com

Art Direction: Stefan Gutermuth
Cover and Interior Illustrations: Maggie Agro
Interior Design: Dianne Nelson, Shadow Canyon Graphics
Page Layout: Cynthia Lamb, using the fonts Granjon and Minion

Distributed by: Publishers Group West, 1700 Fourth Street, Berkeley, California 94710.

Library of Congress Cataloging-in-Publication Data

Gardening among friends : 65 practical essays by master gardeners / edited by Barbara J. Euser.
   p. cm.
 ISBN 1-932361-36-7 (pbk.)
 1. Gardening—Anecdotes. I. Euser, Barbara J., 1949-

SB455.G3554 2006
635—dc22

2006007592

Printed in the United States
10 9 8 7 6 5 4 3 2 1

Contents

~

PREFACE ix

CHAPTER 1: HABITAT GARDENING 1
   Creating the Habitat Garden by Charlotte Torgovitsky 3
   Invite Birds to Visit by William Bentley 6
   Blooms to Attract Hummingbirds by Barbara J. Euser 9
   A Bee or Not a Bee? by Elizabeth R. Patterson 12
   Native Bees as Pollinators by William Bentley 15
   Butterflies in the Habitat Garden by Charlotte Torgovitsky 18
   Birds Welcome Habitat Gone to Seed by Charlotte Torgovitsky 21
   Luring California Quail into Your Habitat by Elizabeth R. Patterson . 24

CHAPTER 2: LOW WATER, LOW MAINTENANCE 27
   Low-Maintenance Gardening by Elizabeth Navas Finley 29
   LuAnn's Garden by Barbara J. Euser 32
   Low-Maintenance Love Affair with Roses by Annie Spiegelman 34
   Plan Water-Wise Garden Before Drought by Lee Oliphant 38
   Xeriscape Fundamentals by Darla Carroll 41
   Ornamental Grasses Set Garden Mood by Virginia Havel 44

CHAPTER 3: FAVORITE FLOWERS AND FOLIAGE 47
   Rosemary Means Remembrance by Barbara J. Euser 49
   Ceanothus Blue by Barbara J. Euser 52
   Forget-Me-Not by Annie Spiegelman 55
   The Elfin Gardens of Mosses, Liverworts and Lichens
      by Virginia Havel 57
   Superlative Salvias by Barbara J. Euser 60
   Awesome Alstroemerias by William Bentley 63
   Exotic Epiphyllums: "Orchids" of the Cactus World by Virginia Havel 65
   Bamboo by Barbara J. Euser 68
   Long-Lasting Lavender by Barbara J. Euser 71
   Easy Orchids: One Inside, One Outside by Katie Martin 74
   Japanese Maples in Your Garden by Julie Monson 76

CHAPTER 4: GARDEN PRODUCE 79
The Less Strenuous Food Garden by Elizabeth Navas Finley 81
Tomatoes by Charlotte Torgovitsky 85
The Fast Food Garden by Annie Spiegelman 88
Pumpkins by Elizabeth R. Patterson 91
Cool Season Vegetables by Diane Lynch 93
Enjoying Herbs Year Round by Sally Lucas 95
Growing Garlic, aka The Stinking Rose by Diane Lynch 98
Savoring the Harvest by Maggie Agro 101
Good Enough to Eat: Safe and Tasty Flowers
    by Annie Spiegelman 104
Asparagus by Elizabeth R. Patterson 107
Olives by Charlotte Torgovitsky 110
You Too Can Grow Citrus by Virginia Havel 114
Persimmons: Fruit of the Gods by Marie Narlock 117
Jujube Dates by Barbara J. Euser 120

CHAPTER 5: GARDEN MAINTENANCE 123
So What Is Organic Gardening? by Diane Lynch 125
What's the Best Mulch for Your Garden? by Jane Scurich 129
Worm Composting in Small Spaces by Lee Oliphant 132
Sheet Composting by Charlotte Torgovitsky 135
Weed Identification and Control by Barbara J. Euser 138
Keep Pests at Bay, Don't Poison Earth by Julie Ward Carter 143
Uninvited Guests by Jane Scurich 146
Foiling Deer Gracefully by Barbara J. Euser 149
Amazing Surviviors: Rats and Mice by Diane Lynch 152
Pruning Shrubs and Vines by William Bentley 156

CHAPTER 6: CYCLE OF SEASONS 159
Putting the Garden to Bed by Maryrose Whelan 161
Fall Checklist for Christmas Blooms by Jane Scurich 163
Clean Your House in the Spring, Clean Your Garden in the Fall
    by Jeanne Price 166
The Leaves Are Falling! by Charlotte Torgovitsky 169
Winter Spraying with Dormant Oil by Jane Scurich 172
Embracing Winter as a Gardener by Darla Carroll 175

~ Contents ~

Care of Gift Plants by Jane Scurich 177

Spring Soil Strategy by Melissa Gebhardt 179

Tiptoe through More than Tulips Next Spring by Melissa Gebhardt . . 182

CHAPTER 7: GARDEN DESIGN 185

The Evolution of a Family Garden by Anita Jones 187

Treehouses: Not Just for Kids Anymore! by Marie Narlock 190

Designing a Garden for Children by Sally Lucas 193

Gardening with a Japanese Touch by Julie Monson 196

Enhancing Wealth through Water Structures by Terumi Leinow 199

Dogs: Delightful or Devious in the Garden by Diane Lynch 201

Gardens Can Keep Memories Alive by Anita Jones 204

APPENDIX: DEMYSTIFYING BOTANICAL NAMES by Julia Flynn Siler . . . 207

AUTHOR BIOGRAPHIES 212

INDEX 219

Preface

~

Gardening Among Friends is a product of the Master Gardener program. Today Master Gardener programs work actively in all fifty of the United States and in Canada. Begun in 1973 in the state of Washington, these programs now involve thousands of volunteers who annually donate hundreds of thousands of hours of their time to improve gardening practices in their communities, spanning the continent.

Master Gardeners receive intense training, sponsored by state universities through the cooperative extension system. After passing a qualifying examination, Master Gardeners volunteer time assisting school and community gardens, lecturing on garden topics, demonstrating gardening techniques, providing telephone diagnostic services, writing gardening columns, and working on other public gardening projects.

Columns written by Master Gardeners for local papers and other publications are an important element of the educational work Master Gardeners perform. Each essay in this collection was written by a Master Gardener and was first published in Northern California's *Marin Independent Journal* as a contribution to the weekly Master Gardener column that has appeared in that paper since 1999.

The information in the essays chosen for this collection applies throughout the country. Each essay reflects the Master Gardener philosophy of relying on native plants and other locally appropriate species, coupled with integrated pest management using less toxic methods of control, to create a healthy garden environment.

In creating this book, I would especially like to thank Katie Martin, editor of the weekly Master Gardener column in the *Marin Independent Journal*, for her assistance in the preparation of the manuscript. I would also like to thank Maggie Agro for her artistic contributions of the cover art and chapter illustrations. Susan Brady of

Solas House Press enthusiastically and tirelessly guided the production of this book to press.

Gardening Among Friends includes essays by twenty-one writers. Each writer uses his or her own voice to discuss a particular aspect of gardening. It is this interplay of ideas and personal experiences—in fact, a conversation—that I like most about this book.

Please join us in our conversation. We invite you to take us into your garden, where we will enjoy the flowers and foliage, birds and insects, water and soil, sky and sun, together.

—BARBARA J. EUSER, EDITOR

~

CHAPTER ONE

~

Habitat Gardening

Creating the Habitat Garden

~

BY CHARLOTTE TORGOVITSKY

My garden is designed as a habitat garden, densely planted in a naturalistic theme to attract birds, butterflies, and beneficial insects. My garden is also an organic, edible garden, for we humans are not to be overlooked as an important part of the habitat garden! I have created a personal connection with this bit of the earth, from the seasonal rhythms and cycles to the constant activity of creatures finding some sustenance in my organic habitat garden.

With a blend of native plants, introduced habitat plants, and a selection of fruit trees, berries, herbs, vegetables, and ornamentals, the garden provides not only for the birds and butterflies that visit, but also for its human occupants. It is a truly edible garden, with beauty and bounty to share.

In spring, the level of activity in my garden crescendos: sparrows, finches, towhees, doves and pigeons empty the bird feeders at a rapid rate. A lot of energy is required to feed fast-growing nestlings. The importance of gardening organically is particularly evident during the breeding season, as all birds rely on insects as a source of protein to feed nestlings that are growing at an astounding rate.

Sheet composting, or a layer of mulch on garden beds, and leaf litter left under trees and shrubs provide ample opportunities for sparrows and towhees foraging for insects. Other species of birds will glean insects directly from plants, providing for their young, and at the same time helping to maintain a natural balance in an organic garden.

Trees and shrubbery, densely planted to create vertical layers, with flowering plants, grasses and vines included in the scheme, all provide cover, nesting sites and foraging opportunities for local bird populations.

Several fruit trees are included in my habitat garden, planted for the pleasure of my family, but in fact, also providing for foraging birds. An Asian pear tree produces many sweet and tasty fruits; those that the birds have sampled are cleaned and processed into a delicious jam. The olive tree, too, provides for scores of birds over a long fruiting season. I pick olives in the red-ripe, or black-ripe stage to cure, leaving some for the birds that eat them in an overripe stage. Larger birds, such as the crows, jays and starlings come to pick the fruit from the tree; many other birds forage from the fruit that has fallen to the ground.

I grow strawberries, too. A raised bed, three feet wide by about eight feet long, has provided my family with delicious fruits from May through September. But there are creatures in the garden that I do not wish to share the berries with: slugs and snails, including the minute black slug that curls itself up in a small hole in the strawberry. Careful spring maintenance eliminates almost all damage from these members of the mollusk family. In early March, I remove all the old leaves from each plant, and renew a third of the bed by removing old plants, and replacing them with vigorous young plants. Around the crown of each plant I sprinkle diatomaceous earth, an organic product that kills crawling insects. Crushed oyster shell is laid down thickly in a wider circle around each plant, to repel soft-bodied crawling pests like the snails and slugs. The bed is irrigated by a drip system and mulched with straw, and I take care never to water from overhead. The occasional raccoon that visits the garden will eat some berries, but there are still plenty of the luscious red-ripe berries for breakfasts, desserts and jam.

Vegetables, both summer and winter crops, are grown in raised beds, and planted among the ornamentals. Basil and Swiss chard are attractive foliage accents among flowering plants; some varieties of hot peppers are attractive ornamentals in their own right, as well as providing for the kitchen. To attract the beneficial insects, flowers such as sweet alyssum, calendula and marigolds are planted among the vegetables in the raised beds. Culinary herbs, too, are planted throughout the garden; they attract many beneficial and pollinating insects, and are good nectar plants for visiting butterflies.

When treated as an ecological system, with yard trimmings and kitchen waste recycled in the form of compost, a garden can provide for itself. Most plant material can be processed into compost, using either active systems, such as a compost tumbler, or passive systems, such as wire bins or sheet composting. A vermicomposting system (composting with worms, see article Chapter Five) can take care of most of the kitchen scraps, and also provides valuable nutrients that can be used to promote healthy, vigorous and productive plant growth, the most basic element in a thriving habitat garden.

Invite Birds to Visit

~

BY WILLIAM BENTLEY

I was in Hawai'i recently and loved waking up to the bird chorus each morning directed by Mother Nature. What a delightful way to start the day! It also reminded me of the important role birds play in our environment. I started thinking about what makes a garden attractive to birds. Their major needs are similar to those of humans—food, water and protection. If we want birds to visit our gardens, we must address these requirements.

FOOD

Birds generally are insect, nectar or seed feeders. In planning your garden, take care to select plants that will provide these things. Native plants will provide the best environment since they are similar to what is found in the wild. Create diversity in your garden by using plants that will provide food at different times of the year, and thus attract a variety of birds. For example, California poppy (*Eschscholzia californica*) blooms and seeds early in the season while cosmos seeds in the fall. Plants should also provide food for both seed and insect feeders. Oaks provide both seed (acorns) and insects as a food source, attracting different birds. Let some flowers go to seed rather than deadheading them immediately, providing additional sources of food. Since birds are very sensitive to insecticides, gardeners should reduce or eliminate the use of toxic chemicals.

Trees that are good for birds are: maples, madrone, strawberry tree, western redbud, toyon, pines, oaks, and elderberry. Shrubs that provide food for birds are: manzanita, ceanothus, cotoneaster, butterfly bush (*Buddleia*), coffeeberry (*Rhamnus californica*), currant and gooseberry (*Ribes*). Many perennials provide food for birds, including columbine, buckwheat, monkey flower (*Mimulus*), penstemon and sage (*Salvia*).

Although my preference is to provide food using natural resources, many gardeners use bird feeders to attract birds. Birds will gravitate to the section of the garden where the feeder is installed. There are many different types of feeders and some are designed for specific birds. Care should be taken when locating the feeder so that the birds will have adequate protection from predators.

WATER

Necessary for drinking and bathing, a good water source goes a long way in attracting and retaining birds in the garden. The movement of water is particularly enticing. As with feeders, the placement of the water source should provide safety from predators. Position it close to protective cover or to areas where the birds can scope out the yard for predators. Don't forget about predators around the neighborhood—cats should have bells to alert the birds to their presence or be kept indoors. In my garden, I have three birdbaths: the first is a traditional birdbath on a pedestal, the second is a shallow bath located on the ground and the third is a small fountain with running water. In some cases, we should be taking reservations!

PROTECTION

The bird habitat should provide adequate cover for feeding, nesting and protection from predators. It should also provide protection from the weather. Diversity is the key to a successful environment. Tall trees and dense shrubs can be used for food and nesting, as well as protection from the wind. An untidy garden may provide the best protection. A pile of old pruning clippings serves as an excellent hiding or nesting place for birds that are ground foragers. If possible, a portion of the garden should be allowed to grow wild, providing a natural setting for your visitors.

Besides being enjoyable to watch, birds help control insects, pollinate flowers and distribute seeds—and their bathing enthusiasm is amazing! I particularly enjoy watching mourning doves and their devotion to each other as they cautiously move through the garden. Welcome all these fascinating visitors to your garden by providing for their needs.

Blooms to Attract Hummingbirds

~

BY BARBARA J. EUSER

John James Audubon called hummingbirds "glittering garments of the rainbow." Attracting these tiny, shimmering birds to our gardens is easy to do and well worth the effort. Most hummingbirds migrate from one location to another during the year, traveling hundreds, even thousands of miles.

Once hummingbirds locate a garden that provides them with food, water, and cover for resting and potential nesting sites, individuals will return year after year. Small as they are, they will aggressively defend their territory against larger birds and other trespassing hummingbirds.

Regarding food sources, hummingbirds are most interested in red flowers with tubular shapes to accommodate their long bills. They are also very efficient pollinators. As they probe deep into the flower for nectar, they pick up pollen on their crowns. The pollen is then transferred to the next flower they approach for food. Thus, planting groupings of one species of flowers that hummingbirds like is beneficial to both birds and plants.

Native hummingbird plants and local hummingbird species have evolved together. The birds prefer reliable native sources of food that will provide for all their nutritional needs. Although cultivated plants such as impatiens have bright flowers, they are not necessarily good sources of the nectar hummingbirds require.

Using a selection of plants, one can provide for hummingbirds throughout the year. It is especially important to provide food in the winter months when not much else is blooming. Flowering currants that bloom in mild climates in winter provide rich nectar for hummingbirds. *Ribes sanguineum* flowers in January and *Ribes malvaceum* blooms through winter into March. Choose the right species for your garden: *R. sanguineum* prefers a dry, sunny location, whereas *R. malvaceum* needs some water. Having planted Ribes species, gardeners can look forward to the annual return of the rufous hummingbird.

Coral bells (*Heuchera maxima*) is an early spring bloomer in my garden that attracts hummingbirds. Hundreds of tiny bell-shaped flowers hang from the two-foot wiry stems. The leaves of the plant form a compact mound and may be divided in the fall. *Heuchera maxima* is native to California's Channel Islands. In addition, there are a number of other species, such as *H. sanguinea*, native of Mexico and Arizona, that also appeal to hummingbirds.

Western columbine (*Aquilegia formosa*) blooms from the spring into the summer. It has scarlet or orange, backward-projecting petals with contrasting yellow sepals and protruding stamens. The flowers nod gracefully on their stems. This species is native in a wide area from Utah to California to Alaska. It thrives in a woodland garden, prefers moist, rich soil and will tolerate filtered shade. In addition to nourishing hummingbirds, allowing columbines to go to seed will provide relished food for song sparrows, juncos and other small birds.

Several species of *Salvia* attract hummingbirds. They are drought tolerant, needing very little water in the summer. Blooming from spring through summer, *Salvia clevelandii* with its whorls of purplish flowers is an exception to the red, tube-shaped generalization. In my garden, I planted *S. clevelandii* for its spicy fragrance, which apparently makes little difference to hummingbirds. Like most birds, hummingbirds don't have much sense of smell. However, they are attracted to its nectar.

Its cousin, *Salvia greggii*, known as autumn sage, does have bright red tubular flowers, and is a notable hummingbird favorite in my garden. To promote flower production and to keep them from becoming too woody, salvia bushes should be cut back annually in the fall. I find this hard to do, but I have learned that it works.

Mexican sage (*S. leucantha*) also blooms in late summer. Its many stems produce vivid purple tubular flowers, which hummingbirds in my garden seem to love. It can be easily divided by digging up clumps of stems and replanting them.

For nectar-rich blooms in the fall, the California native fuchsia (*Zauschneria californica,* renamed *Epilobium*) is one hummingbirds cannot resist. In fact, one of its common names is hummingbird fuchsia. Its inch-long bright red or red-orange tubular flowers bloom at the end of arching stems. This drought-tolerant ground cover thrives in hot, dry summers and will spread by roots and reseeding. In my garden, I encourage its spreading, although *Zauschnerias* have been accused of becoming invasive.

Red-hot poker plants (*Kniphofia uvaria*), natives of South Africa, with their spikes of bright orange red flowers, quickly catch the attention of hummingbirds. This plant adds a vertical note to my garden plantings and is also easily divided.

Other plants that attract hummingbirds include monkey flower (*Mimulus aurantiacus*), firebird penstemon (*Penstemon gloxinioides*), manzanita (*Arctostaphylos*), hummingbird fern (*Grevillea* 'Canberra') and island bush snapdragon (*Galvezia speciosa*).

A Bee or Not a Bee?

~

BY ELIZABETH R. PATTERSON

When is a bee not a bee? Answer: when it is an unwelcome guest at a picnic or barbecue. We commonly use the word "bee" to refer to any flying insect that stings, but the insect attracted to the food on our plates is almost certainly a yellow jacket (*Vespula pensylvanica*), a wasp. How can I be so sure? Unless platters of pollen are being served, honeybees (*Apis mellifera*) have no interest in human food. Yellow jackets, on the other hand, will scavenge for meat, fruit and sweet drinks. Understanding this dietary difference will help us distinguish bees from wasps and understand the very different roles they play in our garden.

Bees and wasps are both members of the insect order Hymenoptera. Within this very large order, there are a great number and variety of wasps and bees, most of which lead inconspicuous, solitary lives. The western yellow jacket and the honeybee, however, attract our attention because of their numbers—both live in colonies which consist of a fertile queen and numerous sterile female workers—and because they both can deliver a painful sting. They sting, however, for very different reasons.

The yellow jacket is a hunter. They hunt other insects to feed to their developing larvae. Their sting can be used repeatedly to paralyze and kill their prey, which they cut into a transportable size and deliver to the nest. In return, the larvae produce honeydew on which the adult yellow jackets feed. Yellow jackets prey on insects that we don't want in our homes and gardens—flies and tomato hornworms, for example—as well as beneficial insects. Yellow jackets find honeybees a particularly tasty treat. They also are attracted to the protein which humans eat, and grilled chicken or hamburgers are easy prey.

By summer's end, female workers outnumber the nectar-producing larvae, and this is when yellow jackets become bothersome. Only fertilized yellow jacket queens survive the winter to start a new colony in the spring. They raise the first brood of female workers who then assume the role of feeding the larvae and expanding the colony. By the end of August, the nest may contain 2,000 to 5,000 workers. After male yellow jackets and next year's queens are raised, the queen stops laying eggs. With no larvae to feed or to produce honeydew, hungry female workers scavenge for carbohydrates to survive.

While yellow jackets are adept hunters, honeybees are best suited for the gathering of pollen and nectar. Around 100 million years ago, flowering plants (angiosperms) and bee ancestors (probably early wasps) developed a wonderful working relationship. The insects fed on nectar and pollen and in the process distributed pollen from one flower to another, assuring fertilization and seed production for the plant. The co-evolution of bees and angiosperms has resulted in a spectacular variety of flowers and insects wonderfully equipped for pollination. Honeybees' bodies are covered with branched hairs to which the pollen sticks, and combs on their legs gather and store pollen into pollen sacks. Honeybee larvae feed on pollen, a source of protein. Honeybees produce a year-round supply of food—honey— from the nectar they collect so that the hive can survive the winter. Honeybees do have a stinger, which they use to defend the hive's honey and larvae, but unlike the yellow jacket, the honeybee dies after stinging just once. Worker honeybees must stay incredibly busy to accomplish the work of the hive, and are too busy to bother the humans in their garden.

As gardeners, we need to support our insect allies. To start, know the difference between bees and wasps. Bees and wasps are both sensitive to pesticides. Spraying throughout the garden will kill pollinating bees as well as unwelcome yellow jackets. To eliminate yellow jackets, focus on finding and eradicating their nests that are most often in the ground. A professional can apply a small amount of pesticide directly to the nest, lessening the impact on other insects in the area. To divert the yellow jackets from your table, prepare them their own meal. Set out a can of tuna cat food in an out of the way location a day ahead of time, and they won't crash your party. Or eat outside at night—yellow jackets do not fly after dark. Honeybees occasionally swarm when they are looking for a new home. Because they do not have a hive to defend and because they are full of honey, swarming bees are usually docile and will stay close to their queen. Do not kill the swarm. It will eventually move on. If necessary, call a professional beekeeper to move them. A rose may smell as sweet when called by another name, but a bee is not a wasp and we should not confuse the two.

Native Bees as Pollinators

~

BY WILLIAM BENTLEY

One of three bites of food we consume depends on the pollination efforts of a bee, butterfly, bat, bird or other pollinator. Although wind and water serve to transport some pollen grains, on a global level over 90 percent of all flowering plants depend on animal pollinators to produce seed. According to Stephen Buchmann, co-author of the book *The Forgotten Pollinators*, "Without pollinators we wouldn't be here. Pollinators are the ecological glue that keep our ecosystem running. Take them out of the picture and everything tends to fall apart."

Recent surveys show that thousands of species are required to pollinate the crops that feed the world. Domestic honeybees service only 15 percent of these crops, while wild bees and other wildlife pollinate at least 80 percent.

Hummingbirds and butterflies may be the most beautiful pollinators and every garden should contain plants to attract them. However, perhaps the most important major group of pollinators is native bees. They are called solitary bees because, unlike honeybees, most operate independently and do not form large colonies. Bumble, carpenter, digger and sweat bees make up the bulk of solitary bees in most parts of the country. These efficient pollinators play a major role in pollinating crops and flowers.

Solitary bees have a number of advantages over honeybees as pollinators. Some of these are that:

- They are active in early spring, before honeybee colonies reach large size.
- They tend to stay in a crop rather than fly between crops, thereby providing more efficient pollination.

- They fly at greater speeds enabling them to pollinate more plants.
- The males also pollinate the crop and are usually gentle.

Bumblebees are classified as solitary bees even though they form small colonies of 1 to 500 workers. However, most solitary bees make their nests in soil or wood. They lay single eggs in divided cells. The eggs hatch and the larvae eat, grow and pupate inside the same cell. The males usually emerge before the females, which are mated immediately after emerging from the cell and the cycle repeats itself.

According to the U.S. Department of Agriculture, we are facing an impending pollination crisis in which both wild and managed pollinators are disappearing at alarming rates due to habitat loss, pesticide poisoning, diseases and pests. We must all be aware that pollination is not free. We must help sustain pollinators.

Provide Nesting Habitat

One of the best ways to preserve native bees is to continue to preserve natural habitat. Parks and public land provide significant open space. In addition, in urban areas, we should strive to maintain open areas and carve out some open space in our home gardens, which can serve as a habitat. Most bees love sun and prefer to nest in dry spaces. For ground nesting bees, this means a sunny patch of open soil. For wood nesting bees, piles of branches will help. For migrating pollinators such as bats, hummingbirds, moths and butterflies, we should strive to maintain habitats on their migratory routes.

Don't Use Harmful Pesticides

Extensive use of pesticides is extremely harmful to bees and other pollinators and has contributed to a substantial decline in their populations. We should urge our counties and cities to practice Integrated Pest Management (IPM) to eliminate or reduce the use of pesticides. We should also use IPM in our home gardens and minimize the use of pesticides. You can obtain information on IPM from your local county extension agent.

Provide Plants for Pollination

One way to attract pollinators in our gardens is to design the gardens with plants that are attractive and useful to pollinators. Many common plants in our gardens serve as a food source for native bees. These include agapanthus, allium, apple, aster, bellflower, ceanothus, penstemon, catmint, plum, apricot, columbine, cosmos, geranium, foxglove, yarrow, and mallow. Planting native plants so that there is a mutual relationship between the plant and pollinator is the best way to ensure adequate native pollinators.

Support Farmers who Support Wild Pollinators

Throughout the United States, there are many organic farmers who do not use pesticides on their crops. We can support them by buying their produce at farmers' markets and local grocery stores.

Butterflies in the Habitat Garden

~

BY CHARLOTTE TORGOVITSKY

Butterflies could be considered the most delicate advertisers of nature's ephemeral beauty. An organic garden full of brilliant, colorful flowers will bring them in to visit, because most rely on nectar as a source of energy. But butterflies, which are *Lepidoptera* in the adult stage, are intent on reproducing the species, and are actually seeking the ideal plant on which to lay their eggs.

This is known as the larval host plant, and it is an essential part of a successful habitat garden. Remember, too, that it is essential to avoid using insecticides in a habitat garden. Insecticides are harmful to all insects: the bad, the beneficial, and the beautiful.

Most butterflies live a brief life in the adult stage, the average life span being just three weeks; they only need to survive in order to reproduce. In the mobile stage of the species, butterflies also colonize new areas. Some are found in a broad range, and some are famous for migrating long distances.

One of the first butterflies we see each year, on warm, sunny days in winter is the Mourning Cloak. This is a large, dark butterfly—brown wings with a line of deep-blue spots, edged with a yellow border. It is widespread throughout North America, and is found in Europe and Asia as well. The Mourning Cloak is unusual in that it lives nearly a year in the adult stage, spending the cold winter days hidden among the trees. With wings folded, its brown coloration conceals it beautifully in the bark and crevices of trees. If your garden contains a willow, elm, or cottonwood, look for the larvae of the Mourning Cloak in March or April.

Native plants are essential to an active habitat garden. Our native plant and insect species have evolved together over thousands of years in mutually beneficial relationships. One of the best native plants for

18

a habitat garden is the sticky monkey flower, a wonderful habitat plant because it supports the larvae of the Common Checkerspot in spring, and provides nectar for hummingbirds in the late summer. The Common, or Chalcedon Checkerspot is found only in California; when hiking, a sharp eye can also find the fuzzy, black larvae on other native members of the Figwort family, such as Indian warrior and Indian paintbrush. The larvae in my garden will often wander and appear sometimes on *Linaria, Penstemon* or *Scrophularia*, also members of the Figwort family.

Some butterflies have very specific host plants for their larvae, others can use a broad range of plants. The Pipevine Swallowtail is a large bluish butterfly that is monophagus, meaning that its larvae can only be sustained by the California pipevine. The California pipevine can be cultivated successfully given moist, shady conditions, and a place to climb. In the wild, the pipevine is often found scrambling up trees and shrubs at streamside, or in the damp redwood forests.

The Anise Swallowtail is a butterfly that is polyphagus. Its larvae can use a broad range of plants and, in fact, it has adapted to plants introduced into its home range. This beautiful black and yellow butterfly uses plants native to North America, such as hog fennel, poison hemlock and purple sanicle to host its larvae. Now the larvae can more often be found on Queen Anne's lace, introduced from Europe and well established throughout the country, and wild fennel.

Bronze fennel is a better choice for the habitat garden, as it is much less invasive. The larvae will also live on dill and parsley. The Anise Swallowtail larvae appear first in late April or May, and, when very small, are camouflaged by a black and white pattern meant to mimic a bird dropping. As they grow, and go through the various instars, the coloring changes to a beautiful pale green, yellow and white striping. They are equipped with forked osmateria, "horns" that the caterpillar quickly extrudes from its head when disturbed, giving off a foul smell to ward off potential predators. The Anise Swallowtail overwinters in the pupal stage, and can remain in that stage for up to seven years if conditions are unsuitable for further development.

All the Swallowtails, as their name would imply, have "tails" at the hind wing. This is an example of back to front mimicry, meant to confuse a predator. If a bird takes a bite out of the hind wing, a butterfly can manage to survive much better than if it suffers injury to its head or thorax.

Birds Welcome Habitat Gone to Seed

~

BY CHARLOTTE TORGOVITSKY

As gardeners, we can make certain choices about how we wish to engage with the plot of land we think of as our garden. As organic gardeners, we choose to emphasize the health of our soils, the plants, and our immediate environment. We use compost, recycling nutrients back to the soil. Growing plants that are healthy enough to resist major insect infestations, we do not use pesticides, but rather, choose plants that attract the beneficial insects that help to establish a natural balance.

As habitat gardeners, we are conservationists on the most personal front, thinking about the native flora and fauna that have evolved together over the millennia, and trying to provide for some of their needs in our own backyards.

We come to the realization that we are simply stewards of a mini-ecosystem that we can create in our backyards. We may think this is "our" garden, but probably more importantly, we are rewarded when "our" garden becomes the territory of a male Anna's Hummingbird.

Anna's Hummingbird is the only hummingbird that we see in Marin the year round. The male claims a rich feeding ground as his territory, and will chase off all other males, but will allow the females to come and feed. During the breeding season he will try to mate with as many females as possible. The richest feeding grounds will entice more females, and thus offer more breeding opportunities.

Hummingbirds are strictly birds of the Americas, and are important pollinators of many of the plants native to the American continents. Salvias, fuchsias, impatiens, penstemons, and iochromas all provide nectar for the hummers. Each species deposits its pollen on a different place on the bird's head, throat, neck, or bill to insure that the pollen is transferred to the correct species, and that fertilization is accomplished.

Once seed is set, *Salvia elegans*, Pineapple Scented Sage, provides for the finches and sparrows as well. House finches and goldfinches both forage for seed on the shrub; white-crowned sparrows forage for seeds on the ground. Many plants are allowed to go to seed in a habitat garden. Fennel, asters, echinacea and other composites all provide seed for the birds in winter. A habitat gardener will wait until spring to cut back the old growth, leaving seed and cover through the winter months.

Many different insects are overwintering in various forms under the bark, on twigs and foliage, and in the leaf litter on the ground. Chickadees, kinglets and bushtits all rely on insects as a staple of their diet. Bushtits come into the garden in flocks of twelve to fifteen: active, tiny birds, gray in color, foraging through the shrubbery with a constant light twittering. They are gleaning insects, moving from one plant to another in a straggling group. They appear in the garden all of a sudden, and move on just as suddenly, having made short work of overwintering insects.

Birds can be our best allies in the organic habitat garden, since many species rely on insects as their main source of food, and all birds, including the hummingbirds, need insects when they are raising their young. Lots of birds also rely on spiders, not just as a food item, but for their webbing, which they use in nest building. The hummingbirds actually use their long bills like a spool to gather strands of spider webbing, and then unwind it to hold together the materials that form their nest. Many spiders, such as the big and beautiful Argiope, a common garden spider, live just one year, leaving a distinctive egg case hidden in a plant, and then dying as the temperatures drop at night.

Winter in California is the rainy season, and the perfect time to get many of our native plants established. Sticky monkeyflower, *Mimulus aurantiacus,* provides nectar for the hummingbirds and butterflies in summer, and is also a larval host plant for several butterfly species. Ceanothus, too, makes a wonderful garden plant with its early bloom of brilliant blue flowers that provide a source of nectar and sustain the larvae of several native species of butterflies.

Perennial wildflowers, such as heuchera, columbine and the blue-eyed grass also provide for the birds and butterflies. Annual wildflowers can be easily established by sowing the seed in place during the winter rains. California poppies, clarkias, baby blue-eyes, lupines, and redmaids all start blooming in early spring when butterfly populations are burgeoning.

Also easily established by seed in the garden are *Impatiens balfouri*, the Poor Man's Orchid, and *Impatiens glandulifera*, the Policeman's Helmet. These charming flowers naturalize easily, in shade or part sun, re-appearing reliably each spring once established in the garden. They provide nectar for the hummingbirds and pollen for the bumblebees, and the deer are not particularly fond of them. So, though not California natives, there is much to recommend them for the habitat garden.

Growing a habitat garden is to engage in the practice of "re-inhabitation," to learn about the land, the native plants and the animals that we live with in our immediate place. It's about receiving sustenance from our plot of land in the form of the fruits and vegetables we can grow for our families, and about providing as much as we can for our native species of birds, butterflies and other insects.

Luring California Quail into Your Habitat

~

BY ELIZABETH R. PATTERSON

It all began when the quail moved into the neighborhood. We would often see them walking warily along the road—father in front with his dark topknot bobbing, followed by mother and scurrying chicks. These California quail were such a pleasurable addition to our neighborhood that I began to wonder how I might attract a family to our yard.

My curiosity about attracting California quail led me to Point Reyes Bird Observatory Conservation Science, a conservation organization dedicated to supporting bird life through research and education. Their website (www.prbo.org) is full of valuable information on creating healthy bird habitat at home. To make our yard attractive to quail, it would need to provide a variety of food, a year-round supply of water and enough heavy growth to provide shelter for nesting and feeding.

To provide food and cover for birds, native plants are always the best choice. In addition to thriving in the local environment, native plants provide food that birds in the area are used to eating and will seek out when foraging. Quail feed principally on seeds of native annuals such as clover, lupine, lotus, filaree, and fiddleneck. But they are not fussy—they also eat fruits, berries, acorns, insects and green foliage.

What is important to quail, and other birds for that matter, are nesting areas that are well concealed. Watering and foraging areas should also be surrounded by dense shrubs and trees for shelter. Native species of trees and shrubs such as red and yellow willows (next to a water source), hazelnut, live oak, snowberry, and wild rose can be planted in clumps to provide shelter. In addition to vegetation,

24

piles of brush left on the ground can be utilized by quail as safe havens.

Quail nest in hollows on the ground, so it is critical that they are protected from predators, especially during their nesting season— mid-March through late July. We do not have a cat, but if we did it would need to live inside. Cats are wonderful pets, but also capable hunters. Scientists estimate that 4 million birds are killed each day in the United States by cats. This unnatural predator places enormous strain on bird populations. For more information on the importance of keeping cats indoors see the American Bird Conservancy website (www.abcbirds.org). Gardeners should also leave nesting areas undisturbed in the spring, so healthy bird habitat is best placed in a quiet corner of the garden that can be left "wild."

So where should this wild, quail-friendly corner of the garden be? The answer came to me while looking out onto a vast patch of periwinkle (*Vinca major*), planted long ago as a low-maintenance ground cover. *Vinca major*, while low maintenance, is also an invasive species, and in our garden it has crowded out the native plants along a stream bank that would have been more attractive to the quail.

It will take a great deal of effort to get the periwinkle up and to replant with native species, and even so, the quail may never find their way to our garden. We will, however, have had the satisfaction of restoring habitat. Loss of habitat, according to PRBO, is one of the main reasons for declining bird populations. In addition, the birds that are attracted to this wild spot will add movement, color and song to what would otherwise be a sea of unchanging green and purple.

Elsewhere in our garden, acorn woodpeckers have made their home in the dead limb of an old oak tree. Their bright red heads attract my attention as they busily collect and store acorns. One day I heard a loud *rat-a-tat-tat* coming from the metal chimney cap on our roof. A male acorn woodpecker was creating a cacophony, which I found out was his way of attracting a mate. The acorn woodpecker had made himself at home in our garden, and someday, hopefully, so will a covey of quail.

Quail did visit our garden, a whole family of them. They first appeared among the native plants, where the California poppies flower in profusion, but soon became comfortable on the lawn, in the vegetable garden and around the pool. I hope that they survived the cats that prowl the neighborhood and enjoyed our garden enough to return in the future.

~

CHAPTER TWO

~

Low Water, Low Maintenance

Low-Maintenance Gardening

~

BY ELIZABETH NAVAS FINLEY

Many people want a colorful garden without spending a lot of time or money to maintain it. To create gardens to meet these seemingly contradictory needs, here are a few strategies.

The most important is to design the garden to suit the existing conditions. Plants that enjoy a shady redwood grove won't thrive on a sunny hillside and vice versa. Go along with your site's character, and the reward is plantings that grow well and resist diseases and pests.

Next, limit lawn areas, because turf grass demands weekly mowing, regular fertilization and aeration. Plant just the amount of lawn needed for frolicking with children and pets and site it where it will get six hours or more of sun daily. Shade causes lawn grasses to thin out and allows weeds to invade.

Not all areas of the garden need to be intensely gardened. Mentally divide your garden into two zones: high-impact areas where color and texture are important (usually around the front walkway and door, back decks and patios and areas seen through windows in major rooms) and low-impact zones, usually outlying areas between the property line and the high-impact areas.

For the high-impact areas, try adding or substituting easy-care plants in the flowerbeds and borders. These are some of my favorites:

+ Neat and Tidy Edgers: If the edges of beds are crisp and tidy, the garden looks well groomed. Try evergreen plants that grow densely to smother weeds, such as sun-loving golden oregano, or shade-loving mondo grass. Shrubs and low hedges also create crisp frames around planting beds while hiding weeds and leaf litter.

- Glamorous Ground Covers: Flowering ground cover plants can substitute for high-maintenance perennials in the flower border. Choose ones with good leaf shape and a bonus of seasonal color, such as the new hybrid *Heuchera* with silver-splashed, burgundy leaves and spikes of delicate flowers. Other glamorous ground covers include *Liriope*, or big blue lily turf, and perennial geraniums like 'Biokovo.' Plant them in large patches—at least nine to thirteen plants—for best display.

- Shapely Shrubs: Look for evergreen, flowering shrubs that grow into fine shapes without much pruning. White-flowered *Choysia*, Mexican mock orange, is one and the *Hebe* is another good group with spikes of white or violet flowers. Colorful *Camellia sasanqua* and upright *Camellia japonica* hybrids are great bloomers that also need little attention.

- Colorful Foliage: Leaves can be as colorful as flowers, and last longer, too. Consider the white-margined foliage of shrubby dogwoods, *Pittosporum* and *Abelia*. There are the golden-edged leaves of *Eleagnus* or *Lamium*, and the burgundy leaves of barberries.

- Dramatic Textures: Plants with distinctive shapes, like grasses, ferns, *Clivia* and New Zealand flax add permanent drama to the garden.

- Easy Hedges: Where a low formal hedge is needed, use a naturally dwarf version of boxwood or *Euonymus* that won't need trimming as often, and for a shallow bed where a tall hedge is needed, substitute a plant that grows upright, not outward, such as *Nandina* or clumping bamboo (the clumpers don't create the problems that running bamboos do).

- Trash-Collecting Ground Covers: For reducing maintenance under trees that drop blossoms and leaves, plant a loose ground cover such as *Lamiastrum* or star jasmine that allows plant debris to fall through to the ground and form a mulch rather than needing to be raked off.

In the low-impact areas of your garden, try this easy-care formula: shrubs plus ground covers plus seasonal bulbs. For example, plant a group of three to five large shrubs, all one kind—such as the beautiful deciduous *Viburnum*, flowering quince or *Ceanothus*. Underneath, cover the ground with two or three kinds of weed-smothering ground cover like Southern sword fern, star jasmine, or coral bells, planted in big patches of one kind. For rough areas where deer prowl, a shrubby ground cover is more durable, something like *Cotoneaster* 'Lowfast,' that stays low and spreads wide.

In addition to the shrubs and ground covers, flowering color comes from seasonal bulbs that naturalize, including spring's Spanish bluebells and summer's *Watsonia* and *Crocosmia*.

To ensure that plants grow well, prepare the soil before planting. Dig and amend with organic matter, and after planting cover the soil with four inches of mulch. After the first two years, don't bother fertilizing, just spread an inch of compost on the planting beds each spring for continued good performance.

The benefits of a low-maintenance garden go beyond saving the gardener time. A garden planted with appropriate plants needs fewer chemical aids to grow, and creates a haven for birds, toads, salamanders, and a host of beneficial creatures who will help you maintain a healthy and beautiful garden.

LuAnn's Garden

~

BY BARBARA J. EUSER

LuAnn Rogers and I often sat together during lectures in our Master Gardener class. During breaks, we would talk about applying what we had learned to our own gardens at home. LuAnn did an especially outstanding job, creating a prize-winning low-water garden.

"My goal was to get rid of the lawn," LuAnn said. So she stripped down the front yard and put paths in it. Then she landscaped it with drought-tolerant plants.

LuAnn chose more than two dozen different perennials to create a habitat garden requiring minimal water to maintain. To add color, she grew a few annuals, hollyhocks, cosmos, and Shasta daisies, from seed. In addition, LuAnn added a rose tree and nearly a dozen rose bushes. These needed more water than the rest of her garden. When she watered them occasionally by hand, she also gave an extra splash to the annuals.

To attract hummingbirds, LuAnn planted purple Mexican bush sage (*Salvia leucantha*) and autumn sage (*S. greggii*). She also planted four different *Penstemons*, montbretia (*Crocosmia crocosmiiflora*), California fuschia (*Zauschneria californica*, renamed *Epilobium*), several strawberry trees (*Arbutus unedo*), and rose-scented geraniums (*Pelargonium graveolens*).

Butterflies are attracted to the twelve-inch-high brick-red yarrow (*Achillea*) LuAnn used as a border. Nearby, she incorporated several different varieties of sedum whose fleshy leaves contrast with the feathery leaves of the yarrow. Butterflies are also attracted to the sea pink (*Armeria maritima*) LuAnn used as a ground cover under a pepper tree, the several different varieties of English and French lavender (*Lavandula*) she planted, and cosmos. Against the fence in the front yard, LuAnn placed a garden bench next to a group of lavender plants; when I sat amongst it, their fragrance washed over me.

Butterfly larvae (caterpillars) need food plants and LuAnn's holly-hocks and roses provide a plentiful supply. It is important not to use any pesticides in a habitat garden since the pesticides kill all insects— including the insects one hopes to attract. LuAnn is happy to have some leaves with holes eaten by caterpillars in her garden, in the hopes that butterflies will soon emerge.

In the back yard, she preserved a strip of lawn, but created a wide border of drought-tolerant habitat perennials. She also added a pond ringed with horsetails (*Equisetum hyemale*). "They may have been a mistake," LuAnn admits. Although she loves how natural they look next to the pond, they are extremely invasive and she has had to rig-orously prune unwanted shoots. Next to the pond is a fig tree, heavily laden with fruit in early September. Her border includes a butterfly bush (*Buddleia*) and a rosemary bush pruned into a bonsai-like tree, both attractive to butterflies.

Other plants in the garden include Shasta daisies ("They reseed themselves and I pull some up like weeds," says LuAnn), society gar-lic, manzanita, and ground covers yerba buena and snow-in-the-summer. Gaura plants flutter like their common name, butterflies-in-the-wind. There are two espaliered vines, a fall-blooming clematis and a purple potato vine. Wooly lambs ears (*Stachys*) provide silvery foliage that contrasts with the green leaves of penstemons and others.

LuAnn's watering schedule was once every third day for twenty minutes. Her drip system used half-gallon emitters. She relied on a generous layer of quarter-inch woodchips as mulch to keep the plants' roots from drying out. As it breaks down, the mulch adds organic matter to the soil. For fertilizer, LuAnn employed the castings of her active colony of worms.

LuAnn and her family have moved to the state of Washington. Even though she no longer lives there, LuAnn's garden will continue to provide pleasure to people and sustenance to butterflies and hum-mingbirds for years to come.

Low-Maintenance Love Affair with Roses

~

BY ANNIE SPIEGELMAN

Roses have always been my weakness. I am the neighbor you witness digging at sunset, sneaking another rosebush into my already over-crowded garden. I am blessed to have forty disease-free English rose-bushes blooming outside of my window at this very minute. On a good day, I think my rose garden replicates Chateau Malmaison. On an off day, I wonder if its seasonal parade of blossoms in giant, multi-hued, non-harmonious shades is causing traffic accidents.

Roses, "Queen of the Flowers," have a reputation of being fussy and needing lots of care. If rosebushes are planted in the correct envi-ronment, that is not the case. It took me three years of scientific experimentation (and ouija board consulting) to become proficient at growing roses.

First I found the location in my yard that received six hours of full sun a day and added well-draining soil. Then I removed the sprin-kler system and installed drip irrigation, studied healthy rose prun-ing techniques and followed a consistent organic fertilizing schedule. My pal Rayford Reddell, author, rosarian, and owner of Garden Valley Ranch Nursery, home of 8,000 roses in Petaluma, California, has a gourmet rose diet. I have now followed it for years and my roses continue to bloom all summer long. You begin feeding your roses in March and continue through October with an organic fertilizer con-sisting of different levels of NPK (nitrogen, phosphorous, and potas-sium), Epsom salt, and fish emulsion. It has been well worth the effort.

In home gardens, where unnecessary toxic chemical pesticides and fungicides are used too frequently, Master Gardeners advocate the use of organic products. Our ecologically based strategy is called

Integrated Pest Management (IPM). Gardeners are encouraged to select methods that provide long-term prevention of pest or disease problems with minimum impact on human health, the environment, and non-target organisms. Pesticides should be used only as a last resort, when careful monitoring indicates they are needed.

Here are some of the most common problems rose growers encounter and solutions:

Powdery Mildew

Recognized by its white to gray powdery growth on leaves, shoots, and buds. Leaves may distort and drop. The fungus is active during warm, dry summer months. Overhead sprinkling during midday may limit disease by disrupting the daily spore-release cycle, yet allowing time for foliage to dry. Pruning, collecting and disposing of leaves during the dormant season may limit infestations, but the spore is airborne. Glossy-foliaged varieties of hybrid teas and grandifloras often are more disease resistant. Plants grown in sunny locations with good air circulation are less likely to be infected. Commercial formulations of Neem oil and a commercial fungicide called Kaligreen have both shown good results against the fungus.

Rust

A fungus favored by cool and moist weather infects rose leaves, leaving small orange pustules. Leaves may drop and discolor. Avoid overhead watering and prune back severely any affected canes. In winter, dispose of any fallen leaves. Low levels of damage may be tolerated without great loss. Preventative applications of fungicides may be used, but must be applied early to show any benefit.

Black Spot

A fungus that produces black spots or fibrous margins on the upper surface of leaves and stems. The fungus requires water, so overhead watering should be avoided. Good air circulation is mandatory.

Remove all infected leaves and stems during the dormant season. Again, a combination of a fungicide and horticultural oil or Neem oil may reduce black spot.

Aphids

Aphids are the most common insect pests on roses. They thrive on actively growing tissue such as buds and shoots, so you will find them often on roses just about to burst into bloom. Insecticidal soaps or Neem oil can also be used. I have had great success with a garden hose using a hard spray of water, and then repeating that satisfyingly vengeful method a few days later. Luckily for us, aphids have many natural enemies: lady beetles, soldier beetles, and syrphid flies. If you don't use toxic insecticides in your yard, your garden has a better chance of attracting natural predators to enjoy the good life of feasting on your rose pests.

Spider Mites

Spider mites cause rose leaves to stipple and yellow. Often webbing may appear or leaves will dry up and fall. Spider mites are best diagnosed with a hand lens. They are the size of a dot. Once again, conserving natural enemies is a must. The use of the insecticide, Sevin, applied to control other pests, has reportedly resulted in *increased* mite populations. Insecticidal soaps or horticultural oils have shown good results in controlling the spread of spider mites.

Thrips

Thrips cause injury primarily to rose flowers, causing blossom petals to streak with brown or become distorted. The tiny yellow or black insect hides within the blossoms. Thrips seem to be attracted to fragrant, light-colored, or white roses. In most home gardens, thrips can be tolerated. Frequent clipping and disposal of spent blooms can help reduce thrips damage. Use of pesticides is strongly not recommended since they cannot penetrate within the bud. On a positive note, western flower thrips can be beneficial in your garden since they are a predator of spider mites.

My rosebushes now stand on their own. They fight off attacks from aphids with aphids' natural enemies such as lady beetles, or quickly recover from a bout of powdery mildew before I have to wear my "doting-worried-mother" cap. My roses have become basically self-sufficient. They do their thing. I do mine. They bloom profusely in the spring. I take all the credit.

Plan Water-Wise Garden Before Drought

~

by Lee Oliphant

During winter, water conservation is probably the last thing on your mind. We experienced the wettest December in decades. We went sunless for weeks. Our feet were damp on Thanksgiving Day and soggy on New Year's. We had a reprieve from the dreaded "drought year."

But droughts are cyclical. During drought years, we carried buckets of shower water to our trees and shrubs. Our vegetable gardens lay dormant. We planted no new perennials. The planting of annuals was put on hold for several years. To add insult to injury, our neighbors replaced their lawns with lava rock and never went back to growing green things!

Water is a finite resource, especially in the western United States. Good gardeners are not shortsighted. We look to the future. We plan, design, and envision the lush growth just around the seasonal corner. Now is the time to plan your landscaping and to improve your irrigation system so that when the inevitable cloudless days arrive, you and your garden will survive.

In planning your garden and its water supply, first take into account your local climate. I live in a Mediterranean climate (rain in winter, little to none in the summer). Plants from this region expect wet winters and warmer, dry summers. Wherever you live, there are some specific things you can do to reinforce your garden's resistance to drought:

- Evaluate your site. Know your soil type, sun exposure differences, and slopes and areas where water runoff can be problematic.

- Choose the right plants for the right places. Consider your type of soil (clay, loam, sand), exposure (sun, shade, temperature), water requirements, role of plant (screen, background), characteristics (evergreen, deciduous, flowering) and height, texture, and shape. Extensive plant lists are available from University Cooperative Extension Services throughout the country. Water districts provide information on drought-tolerant plants, for example, the Arizona Department of Water Resources (www.azwater.gov) and Contra Costa Water District, California (www.ccwater.com).

- Group plants by water needs to avoid overwatering those that need very little water to thrive.

- Investigate and consider plans to improve your present irrigation system, or install a new low-usage water system. A drip system works well in many situations and can be easily revised and expanded each year as your garden matures and changes.

- Limit your turf area. Lawns are thirsty. Lawns are responsible for as much as half of outdoor residential water use and many lawns are overwatered. When possible, replace lawns or strips of lawns with ground covers or drought-tolerant grasses.

- Irrigate efficiently to avoid runoff and overspraying. To find out how much water your sprinklers apply, place five straight-sided cans or cups around your lawn or sprinkled area. Run sprinklers for at least fifteen minutes. Check cans to see if there is uniform delivery of water. Set timer or manually water only as needed.

- Improve your soil with organic matters such as compost. This helps the soil to retain moisture.

- Cover ground with mulch to reduce moisture loss, reduce weeds, and to eventually enrich the soil. Mulches that are commonly used are compost, aged sawdust and shredded bark and are applied to a depth of four inches.

- Keep your watering system in good working order. Monitor the system on an ongoing basis. Check your automatic timer and change the allotted time as appropriate. Check plants regularly using a soil probe to monitor soil moisture. Remember, water requirements usually decrease as the days shorten.
- Container plants need special care in the conservation of water. Water-holding polymers can be mixed into the soil of pots to help retain moisture. Double potting (setting small pots inside larger ones with a layer of sand or gravel between them) will help keep pots cool and moist. Compost over the soil surface of plants in containers.

Being water-wise does not mean that you have to give up having a lush garden. There is an abundance of beautiful flowers, foliage plants, shrubs and trees that thrive in a low-water environment.

Xeriscape Fundamentals

~

by Darla Carroll

A surprising amount of water is used in the home landscape. Of residential water usage, almost half is used to maintain the landscape—and a lot of this is wasted. A xeriscape can reduce landscape water use by 70 percent or more.

The term xeriscape is an often-misunderstood concept of landscaping. Xeriscape is not a boring monoculture of spiny plants. On the contrary, well-planned xeriscapes are splendid examples of beauty and diversity in any garden style.

A xeriscape is a landscape that uses plants that have low water requirements, making them able to withstand extended periods of drought. Xeric landscapes are a conscious attempt to develop plantings that are compatible with the environment and reduce water waste.

Here are some common misperceptions:

- Xeriscape doesn't mean only dry. Limited areas that use more water are completely consistent with wise water use.
- Xeriscape is not just rocks and gravel. By definition, xeriscape means some water applied in well-controlled amounts and locations in the landscape.
- Xeriscape is not necessarily "lawn-less" landscaping. Instead, it is a wise choice of grass species and "less lawn" landscaping.
- Xeriscape doesn't use only native plants. Although native plants are a wonderful choice, the idea is to use plants that are well adapted to our local climate.

There are seven fundamentals in xeriscaping:

1. Incorporate zonal planting. With this concept, the high water-requiring plants are planted close to the house in the "oasis

41

zone." A moderate or regular zone would contain plant materials that, after establishing themselves, would require only occasional watering during extended drought periods. The "no water zone" would include native plant species that have adapted to local precipitation patterns. Here, plants would need water for the first year, usually through a drip irrigation system to become established, and then allowed to go entirely on their own. With the three zones clearly defined, it is obvious that three entirely different classes of plant materials will be needed. This takes careful thought in planning and planting to avoid a hodgepodge design.

2. Create practical turf areas of manageable sizes and shapes and with appropriate grasses.

3. Select plants with low water requirements and group plants of similar water needs together. Then experiment to determine how much and how often to water the plants.

4. Use soil amendments like compost or manure appropriate to the site and type of plants used. Generally, natives, grasses and shrubs do not need as highly fertile a soil as most perennials.

5. Use mulches, such as wood chips, to reduce evaporation and to keep the soil cool, to provide nutrients slowly, to change the chemistry of the soil and its physical structure. It should be fairly low cost, as mulch needs to be added on a regular (annual or semi-annual) basis because of microbial breakdown. Mulches that do not break down are not doing their job. Fiber cloth is a much better bet than plastic. The shredded bark called gorilla hair is not advisable, since it packs down and forms an almost impenetrable layer that does not break down easily.

6. Irrigate efficiently with properly designed systems (including hose-end equipment) and by applying the right amount of water at the right time. Call your local water district for its automated water tip line to get a weekly watering schedule.

7. Maintain the landscape properly by mowing (not too low), weeding (lots—but it will be easier if you mulch), pruning

(not too much, instead plant the correct size plant for the space) and fertilizing (usually not as often as you think, especially if you prepared your soil with good amendments).

Planning your landscape with water conservation in mind can save a lot of time and energy, *and* you will save on water bills.

Ornamental Grasses Set Garden Mood

~

BY VIRGINIA HAVEL

The Grass Family includes many useful and diverse plants that grow in all parts of the world. In the past, grasses have been used in gardens mainly for lawns and turf, but more recently landscapers have discovered the unique advantages of incorporating both native and cultivated varieties of grasses into their horticultural designs. Increased demands for attractive new grasses have resulted in a huge variety available in the nursery trade. The artist landscaper has become aware that the special qualities of grasses can create a mood of peace and serenity or a sense of oneness with nature in the garden. Grasses have provided a new dimension of experiencing the garden with all one's senses, not just colorful floral displays.

SOME SPECIAL QUALITIES OF GRASSES

What are some of the special qualities of grasses? They are easy to grow and many are drought and deer resistant. Perennial bunch grasses have lovely rounded shapes, surviving and replacing themselves for many years. Annual grasses re-seed year after year and are attractive when dry in the fall and winter. The blades and flowering stalks are soft tones of greens and blues, subtle mauves and rusts, gold and yellows. In the fall, tans and browns predominate. Variegated white and cream-striped leaves accent some grass plants. The swaying of grasses in the breeze adds movement, a hypnotic rhythm like the ripples on a lake. And after the foliage dries and seeds ripen, the gentle rustling sounds enhance the visual effect.

Size and form of grass plants vary from tiny rock garden mounds to giant bamboo, suitable for shade and hedges. Grasses may be evergreen or long lasting with persistent colorful dried flowers. Some grasses love a wet environment while others are drought tolerant. There are grasses to fill the needs of all landscape requirements.

SEDGES, RUSHES AND OTHER RELATED PLANTS

Grass gardens usually include sedges *(Cyperus)* and rushes *(Juncus)* from closely related families, and other plants with grass-like qualities: horsetails (*Equisetum*), cattails (*Typha*), and New Zealand flax (*Phormium*). Rushes have solid spike-like stems, and sedges often have umbrella-like arrangements of the inflorescence (collective for all the flowers). The classification of grasses, sedges and rushes is based on small flower structures and may require microscopic observation of minute differences. Familiarity with scientific terms of grass morphology is also helpful.

LANDSCAPING WITH GRASSES AND GRASS-LIKE SPECIES

Some native grasses and sedges are excellent as ground covers. The best choices for lawn substitutes are evergreen plants, low growing, with dense foliage that can withstand traffic, and preferably that require little water. Other ground cover grasses may be used for meadows. Grasses about eight to eighteen inches high, closely spaced and mixed with wildflowers or bulbs, are suitable for open areas of gardens. Some recommended species are: *Carex pansa*, California meadow sedge, *C. dolichostachya* 'Kaga Nishidi,' a Japanese variegated form, *C. morrowii*, a cream-edged cultivar called 'Ice Dance,' and a California native, Berkeley sedge (*C. tumulicola*).

For a rock garden, grow mounded forms with flower spikes in bloom at different seasons. Most alpine species will do well. Japanese gardens feature carefully selected rocks placed with colorful grasses such as blue gama (*Bouteloua gracilis*), striped orchard grass (*Dactylis glomerata* 'Variegata'), most fescues, and annual and perennial fountain grasses.

Grasses and grass-like plants that require a wet habitat are attractive near a pond, fountain or natural seep. A sunken tub filled with rock and water is an easy way to create this wetland effect. Plant umbrella plant (*Cyperus alternifolius*), horsetail (*Equisetum hyemale*), bulrush (*Scirpus cernuus*), and cattail (*Typha augustifolia*) in and around pools. Incidentally, the reedy horsetail species is very attractive as filler in cut floral arrangements.

Large showy plantings add focus and are sculptural showpieces in the garden. Pampas grass has long been popular, appreciated for its large white plumes. Unfortunately, it is no longer recommended due to its invasive nature. Even the self-sterile species still available is thought to become fertile under certain circumstances. If you live near any parks or open spaces, avoid all these *Cortaderia* species. *Pennisetum* and *Miscanthus* cultivars of fountain grass are noteworthy for their large cascading leaves and showy flowers. The flowers of Zebra grass (*Miscanthus sinensis*) last late into winter.

Containers of all types, planted with the appropriate grass, are a wonderful way to show off their special qualities. The planter can be moved to the spot in the garden that needs accenting at the right time. If you can place a container in a location to receive back-lighting, you will discover the striking colors and textures of your featured grass.

CHAPTER THREE

Favorite Flowers and Foliage

Rosemary Means Remembrance

~

BY BARBARA J. EUSER

"There's rosemary, that's for remembrance; pray, love, remember."
—*William Shakespeare,* Hamlet, *Act 4, Scene 5*

For centuries, rosemary (*Rosmarinus officinalis*) has been appreciated as a symbolic, medicinal and culinary herb. A native of the Mediterranean region, rosemary thrives in a range of climates. It has many virtues.

Rosemary is a shrub with needle-like leaves and tiny blue flowers that bloom in spring. It is one of the first plants to flower in my garden and different varieties range in color from medium blue to white. It is known for attracting adult butterflies. Bees use the nectar to produce flavorful honey.

Rosemary thrives in tough growing conditions. It can tolerate hot sun and ocean spray. It is drought tolerant once established and can withstand windy conditions. It roots create a dense network that controls erosion on hillsides.

In my garden, rosemary is particularly valuable because the deer do not eat its sharp, stiff leaves. Different varieties perform different functions on our hillside. In one area, I planted *R. officinalis* 'Prostratus' which spreads lavishly across the ground. It is a low shrub and serves as an effective ground cover. Its branches twist and turn back upon themselves, creating interesting shapes and forms.

Near the fence, I planted *R. officinalis* 'Tuscan Blue.' This is an upright shrub and is developing into an attractive hedge. Originally, I had planted one of them near a walkway, an inappropriate spot. After a year or so, it grew too tall and I decided to transplant it. Because of their extensive root systems, rosemary plants are not

49

generally good candidates for transplanting. I nearly killed this one. However, even though about half of the plant died, within a couple of years, it managed to return to vigorous growth—a testimony to the tough character of the species.

Above a low wall, I planted several *R. officinalis* 'Huntington Carpet.' This is a cultivar of the *prostrate* variety. It has deep-blue flowers and will eventually drape down over the wall. This newly landscaped area is under a venerable oak tree. Rosemary, because of its low water requirements, is suitable for planting under oaks. However, again I may have made a mistake. Beneath the wall is a graveled landing with French café table and chairs. My intention is to enjoy lunch in the shade of the oak. I have already noticed that when the rosemary is blooming, insects that were intially attracted to the blossoms are equally attracted to my sandwich.

Being able to propagate plants in my garden gives me special pleasure. Rosemary is an especially good candidate. It can be propagated either by stem cuttings or layering. For stem cutting, take a four- to five-inch sprig of healthy new growth from the top of the plant and root it in moist sand. It will be ready for planting in soil in approximately six weeks. To layer, use a wire staple to peg a branch to the ground and mound soil over it. This is best done in fall or winter when the rains will promote new root growth. By summer, the new plant can be clipped from the mother plant and carefully moved.

There are many uses for fresh rosemary. As a culinary herb, it can be chopped and added to butter for a savory accompaniment to rolls. If one is more ambitious and baking, the chopped herb can be added directly to bread dough, one tablespoon to each loaf. It can be added to fruit salads to enhance sweetness. I sprinkle it over new potatoes when I roast them in the oven. Rosemary leaves are typically added to pork and lamb dishes. When grilling salmon, I place a branch of rosemary on a sheet of foil under the fish.

Sprigs of rosemary can be added to hot bathwater which releases the leaves' essential oil. Its leaves may also be used to brew a tea reputed by herbalists to serve as a tonic, astringent, and to alleviate headaches.

Because it keeps its leaves year round, rosemary is a symbol of fidelity and remembrance. It is used in bridal wreathes and bouquets for its symbolic value as well as its beauty. At funerals, mourners toss sprigs into the grave to signify they will not forget their loved one.

Ceanothus Blue

~

BY BARBARA J. EUSER

Driving through Tiburon yesterday, I passed a small tree covered in purple blossoms. It was a ceanothus, possibly *Ceanothus arboreus*, that is tree ceanothus, which grows either as a dense shrub or can be pruned to develop one main trunk. Ceanothus is native to the western United States and, besides being beautiful in spring covered with purple or white blossoms, has adapted to tolerate a wide variety of climates. It is also known as wild lilac, with blossoms in a similar, miniature form.

Over thirty species of *Ceanothus* grow in many shapes and sizes, though all can be classified as perennial shrubs. With their showy flowers, ceanothus attract hummingbirds and butterflies. They are a fine addition to a habitat garden. In my garden, consciously emphasizing natives and habitat-creating plants, I have planted four different species, for different purposes.

Ceanothus do not require summer water, which make them appealing for that reason alone. In fact, their greatest enemy is overwatering and they may succumb to the water mold Phytophthora. They are therefore suitable for planting under oaks, a major consideration in my garden. Under a venerable old oak in our lower garden, I have planted *C. griseus horizontalis* 'Carmel Creeper.' Its shiny dark-green round leaves are what first attracted me. The fact that it is blooming with tiny purple panicles at the end of February adds to its charm. My garden is separated into an upper and lower section by a tall fence. The upper garden is open to the deer that are frequent visitors. The lower garden is protected from their grazing. Deer like to eat various varieties of *C. griseus*, including Carmel Creeper, so I planted it below the fence.

Under another oak in the lower garden, I planted *C. hearstiorum*. This flat-growing species was discovered on the grounds of Hearst Castle and is reputed to be an endangered species. I could not resist the opportunity to plant some in my garden, although is it considered an undependable performer. But so far, so good. It grows in a star shape and has spread quickly across the slope under the oak. It is not a thick ground cover and some weeds do appear between its branches, but I am very happy with it. It will be blooming soon.

In the upper garden, I recently planted a strip of garden beside steps that lead up to an oak tree growing next to our street. Here, I had to consider plants that do not appeal to deer. Already in place were fortnight lilies, *Dietes*, with their stiff, swordlike leaves, divisions of lilies from elsewhere in the garden. Likewise, I had planted clumps of sword ferns, also taken from a mother plant along this side of the house. I lined the steps with variegated-leafed allium. Against the fence, I planted two different varieties of ceanothus that have prickly holly-type leaves and do not appeal to deer. As a background shrub, I chose *C. thyrsiflorus* 'Skylark.' The deer have avoided it to date. It may grow up to six feet tall and five feet wide.

Several varieties of ceanothus are also effectively used on slopes for erosion control. On my slope, I planted a prostrate ceanothus with small, leathery leaves. It is a perfect candidate for covering a steep, dry open bank. Although its leaves are not prickly, they are not very succulent, so I am hoping the deer will choose something else for snacks.

Ceanothus are susceptible to several pests. One of the most common—and quite serious—can be the ceanothus stem gall moth that causes spindle-shaped swellings (galls). Infestation may cause serious dieback. Spring is the time of year to look for these swellings. Clip them off and dispose of them. It is very important not to drop them on the ground—moths will emerge. Another pest is the lace bug (*Ceanothus tingids*). Ceanothus may also be attacked by oyster shell scale, which unfortunately is not easy to control.

Ceanothus are relatively short-lived shrubs—between four and ten years. They cannot compete against some invasive species. In a passage in her book *Gardening with a Wild Heart*, Judith Lowry imagines a day when our native ceanothus have been replaced by aggressive, invasive broom: "There will be no honey-sweet fragrance emanating from fragile ceanothus blossoms, no strange dry black seeds dropping in midsummer. Tortoiseshell butterflies will not be laying eggs on shiny ceanothus leaves, nor will the ceanothus moth make its cocoons, prized rattles for traditional dances. There will be no swishing the blossoms in a bucket of water to make suds to wash with, as the Pomo did, and wreaths made for the Strawberry Festival will no longer include ceanothus. There will just be yellow." That would be a sad day indeed.

We can make sure they don't disappear. Ceanothus are worthy additions to our gardens as native, drought-tolerant, deer-resistant (some species) shrubs, with flowers attractive to insects and birds as well as to us.

Forget-Me-Not

~

BY ANNIE SPIEGELMAN

While doing my weekly late-winter garden check, I passed patches of weeds that have managed not only to thrive all around my rose-bushes, but to vigorously creep right through the cracks of cement and brick garden pathways. I said some really, really bad words to myself. Then I noticed an area of the garden that had managed to successfully compete with the weeds. It was near the backyard bird-bath and the space was filled with a carpet of sweet *Myosotis*, Forget-Me-Not, in full bloom. Annual Forget-Me-Not, or *Myosotis sylvatica*, are low-growing plants with clusters of tiny blue flowers with yellow centers on fragile, multi-branched stems.

In the late 1700s, the pastor Chris Sprengel became interested in Forget-Me-Not because of their color combination. Blue and yellow flowers are the colors that most attract insect pollinators. Sprengel later left his pastoral duties to pursue botany. He published *The Newly Revealed Mystery of Nature in the Structure and Fertilization of Flowers*, which suggested that all nature had a connected purpose. His peers received it unenthusiastically. Fifty years later, Charles Darwin read the book, recognized the truths in it, and incorporated them in his own research.

Forget-Me-Not spread prolifically each year and are a welcome source of early spring bloom. They reseed themselves generously and look lovely in clumps amongst spring bulbs. They provide a great ground cover, six to twelve inches in height and spread ten to twelve inches wide. In our yard, they compete well with weeds that manage to come back, uninvited, after the winter rains. In mild climates, they bloom from early spring to early summer. Seeds can be sown outdoors in the fall for springtime bloom. Plants thrive best in light, cool shade where they are protected from hot sun, and in rich soil. *Myosotis* do not require fertilizing and need little watering, about one inch of water per week.

They are carefree plants that are seldom bothered by diseases or pests. They do not tolerate summer heat and will become ragged looking or die out completely as soon as the weather turns hot. It is best to shear them back once warm weather arrives. In early summer, when they begin to look dried out, they can easily be pulled out, and a summer annual such as impatiens can be planted in the empty spot.

Although the flowers are tiny, they make great additions to miniature bouquets. I prefer to fill up mason jars with *Myosotis* and place them in rooms throughout the house. Pick the flowers in the early morning and place them directly in cool water.

Myosotis scorpioides is a perennial variety of Forget-Me-Not. It has an even longer blooming season than *M. sylvatica* and the roots live over from year to year. It grows lower to the ground than *M. sylvatica* and spreads by creeping roots.

Another appealing attribute of *Myosotis* is that deer don't like to eat it.

Over the years I have developed a universal botanical *"Whaaa-whaa"* rating system:

Blooms and asks little of the gardener: 1

Hungry, thirsty, needy, and cranky: 10.

Based on my system, I give *Myosotis sylvatica* a *"Whaaa-whaa"* rating of 2.

Myosotis are a great long-term garden investment. One six-pack will reseed for years to come. Go get one!

The Elfin Gardens of Mosses, Liverworts and Lichens

~

BY VIRGINIA HAVEL

Mosses, liverworts and lichens are probably growing in your garden now, and they don't require any care. They live attached to rocks, tree trunks, old sheds and fence posts. These tiny non-flowering plants are not often mentioned in garden books, but they are beautiful, play important ecological roles and serve some useful purposes. All it takes to discover this elfin world is to get down close to the plants and investigate them, preferably with a hand lens.

Mosses and liverworts are called "lower" plants on the evolutionary scale because they lack a vascular system. They were the first plants to colonize land, and never developed true roots, stems, leaves or flowers. Water and nutrients are transferred from one cell to the next. Lack of a vascular system has limited their size and complexity.

Moss plants with flat leaf-like blades spiraling along a stem usually are either male or female. The male plants produce sperm that swim to the female plant in dew or raindrops. A new plant grows from the fertilized egg in the female, but this is a dependent plant quite unlike its moss parent, consisting of a stalk supporting an oval capsule. When the capsule splits, microscopic spores are released and germinate in moist locations into new leaf mosses. This two-staged reproductive pattern is called "alternation of generations." Liverworts have a similar life cycle, but are flat plants with leaves arranged in chain-like patterns. There are thousands of species of mosses and liverworts. Not all plants with moss in their names are really mosses, for example, moss campion (*Silene*), moss pink (*Phlox*), and Irish and Scotch moss (*Sagina*). These are all flowering plants with low-growing, mosslike form. Reindeer moss and Spanish moss are also misnomers: one is a lichen in the tundra, and the other, a flowering plant in the pineapple family, looks rather like netting hanging from tropical trees.

Mosses play important ecological roles as soil formers and aid in water retention and erosion control. Sphagnum is a moss with important economic value. Peat is harvested from sphagnum bogs of northern climates. It is a useful material for packing nursery stock because of its capacity to hold moisture. Sphagnum is also used as mulch for plants and seedbeds. In Ireland, peat has been used as a fuel for centuries.

Lichens are one of the strangest organisms of the plant world. They are actually two different kinds of plants (fungi and algae) combined to benefit both. Algae (either a single-celled, free-living species or bacteria-like blue-green algae) become incorporated into the fungal body. Both organisms benefit from living together. Since the fungus lacks chlorophyll, it requires algae to produce nutrient carbohydrates by photosynthesis. Algae gain a moist, protected environment inside the fungal body, obtaining water and minerals from the fungus.

Lichens can survive in harsh, cold environments, often with little water and nutrients. They are pioneers on bare rock, breaking and dissolving the rock surface and initiating the formation of soil on which mosses and other plants can gain a foothold. The growth form of lichens is dependent on the species of fungus and the characteristics of the algae. Crustose lichens are tightly adhering, thin coverings on rocks, trees, and woody shrubs. Foliose lichens are also found on many surfaces and have a leafy three-dimensional shape. Fruticose lichens are multibranched lichens that hang in long chains from tree branches. Lichen-covered rocks and cliff surfaces make up some of the most beautiful displays in nature. Colors vary from brilliant reds, yellows, oranges, mauves, blacks, grays, creams and whites, chartreuse-greens to soft gray-greens. The reproductive structures, called fruiting bodies, often take on sculptural forms such as cups, club-shapes, buttons and branching stalks. Little is known about the sexual reproduction of lichens, but it entails the release of spores from the fungus that need to capture free-living algal cells to survive. Asexual reproduction by soredia (powder-like particles), containing both fungal threads (*hyphae*) and algae cells, is more dependable, but does not allow for genetic variation.

Many animals rely on lichens as an energy source. Caribou, deer, grouse, and wild turkey graze on lichens. Birds often use lichens in building their nests. Certain insects use lichens for camouflage, and some store lichen chemicals in their tissues as deterrents against predators. Lichens can absorb many kinds of pollutants, including metals and radioactive compounds, and thus can be used as bio-indicators. Some lichens are sensitive to pollutants in cities. Loss of lichens in parks indicates a decline of air quality. Throughout history, lichens have served useful purposes for humankind. Their musk-like fragrance has provided the bases for perfumes and cosmetics. Medicines of all kinds have been made from lichens, and today companies are screening for new pharmaceutical products from lichens. In emergencies, lichens may even be a food for humans. Today lichens are mainly appreciated for their beauty in nature and in gardens. Mosses, lichens and liverworts all add color and texture. They soften harsh rock and wood surfaces and provide a charming quality to our landscape.

Superlative Salvias

~

by Barbara J. Euser

Growing up near Denver, Colorado, I knew salvia only as the bright red spikes of annuals in municipal flowerbeds. It wasn't until many years later that I learned the number and variety of plants the genus *Salvia* includes! Salvias belong to the mint family Lamiaceae. Their leaves are delightfully pungent and many are ornamental as well.

Salvia splendens, of my childhood memories, was introduced to Europe around 1800 by Baron Alexander von Humboldt, the German aristocrat who sent home many plants from his travels in South America. A perennial in its native Brazil and Mexico, it is often grown as an annual further north. Some gardeners find its scarlet too gaudy, whereas hummingbirds love it.

Medicinal Herb

Another common salvia, *S. officinalis,* has been appreciated as a medicinal herb for centuries. A European native, its name derives from the Latin word *salvus,* meaning healed or saved, and *officinalis,* meaning it was on the official list of medicinal herbs. In this context, during the Middle Ages it was reputed to have marvelous healing powers, effective against fevers, sore throats, typhoid fever, headaches, flatulence and many other complaints. Its common name is sage and no herb garden was without it.

Today, *S. officinalis* is better known as a culinary herb, although this use may have originally stemmed from its medicinal properties. According to one source, sage was first added to stuffing for turkeys, sausages and pork dressing to counteract the indigestion that may be caused by these rich, greasy foods. Though we may have forgotten the original purpose, we like the taste. Sage is a welcome addition not only to meat dishes, but also to leafy salads. Its fresh, green leaves can be brewed into a soothing tea. The Chinese are reported to have valued sage tea so highly that they would trade many pounds of their own tea for one pound of sage. Other salvias used as seasoning for food include Cleveland's sage (*S. clevelandii*) and pineapple sage (*S. elegans*), recommended for use in cool drinks and fruit salads.

Widespread and Tough

Salvias are widespread. Over sixty species of *Salvia* grow in the United States. They range from creeping ground covers (*S. sonomensis*) to bushes seven feet tall (*S. uliginosa*). Flower colors range from white to red to purple and shades in between. Many are popular because they are drought tolerant and deer resistant. The salvias in my California garden thrive in clay soil, a definite plus. However, perennial salvias' root areas are sensitive to cold temperatures and should be well mulched before winter. If you decide to grow salvias from seeds, expect that they will germinate slowly, taking two to three weeks. One source suggests that some salvias' roots may be lifted in the fall and stored in moist sand over winter. The new start from roots is reportedly more magnificent than from seeds.

One of the most frequently seen salvias in the San Francisco Bay Area is Mexican bush sage (*S. leucantha*). It grows to three or four feet with graceful, arching stems of velvety purple spikes. In the fall, some say old stems should be cut to the ground. New shoots will emerge in the spring and a single plant will evolve into a colony. In my experience, drastic pruning has been very stressful to the plants and some have taken a full season to recover. Mexican sage transplants well and I have dug up and replanted several sections of a colony, a very effective form of propagation.

Autumn sage is also a three- to four-foot bush. I bought one and was so pleased with its small green leaves and bright red flowers that seemed to go on blooming forever, I bought two more. I didn't realize that there are many colors of *S. greggii*—these two had magenta flowers and the bushes grew into altogether different shapes.

Creeping sage (*S. sonomensis*), as its name implies, is a low-growing ground cover. Its flower stems reach upward with violet blossoms in a spike of whorls. Creeping sage thrives on dry slopes in chaparrel and woodlands. It roots frequently along its stems. It may be too invasive for some gardens, but as a fast-growing, drought-tolerant ground cover, in some situations it may be useful. I plan to try it on a south-facing, lightly-shaded slope, hoping it will spread.

Hummingbird sage (*S. spathacea*) grows two to three feet tall from creeping rhizomes. The purplish red tubular flowers appear in whorls and are very attractive to hummingbirds. It grows easily from seed and volunteers may proliferate. A large, coarse plant, it may be used among other large perennials or in a background planting.

Cleveland's sage (*S. clevelandii*), also called fragrant sage, is a rounded three-foot shrub which grows wild on dry slopes. On a warm day, its fragrance floats beyond it on the breeze. I first encountered it by Muir Beach and immediately bought some for my garden. Whenever I walk by one, I pick a leaf for the pleasure of crushing it for its perfume.

Another California native, black sage (*S. mellifera*) has been variously described. Glenn Keaton, in *Native Shrubs of California*, calls it "perhaps the least attractive [sage]", however "excellent for bees." Judith Lowry, in *Gardening with a Wild Heart*, suggests using black sage as a "keynote plant, to be repeated throughout the garden, [to] give a garden 'bones,' a structure that the eye can follow throughout."

From annual bedding plants to kitchen herbs to the bones of a garden, salvias are most versatile and useful. Consider the valuable additions they could make to your garden.

Awesome Alstroemerias

~

BY WILLIAM BENTLEY

Some of my favorite garden flowers are members of the genus *Alstroemeria*, most commonly called Peruvian lilies. They are also known as Inca or Chilean lilies. As the common names imply, they are native to South America. I just can't resist the beautiful flowers in nurseries. As a result, my garden is full of them. They have umbrella-shaped clusters of three to eight large, flared blossoms, brightly colored and often flecked with darker shades. There are many colors to choose from. The stems are set with whorled or scattered, narrow green to dark green leaves and can grow three to five feet tall. Dwarf plants are also available in a multitude of colors. From late spring through the early fall, they provide quite a show in my garden.

Alstroemerias are excellent cut flowers, as they can last two to three weeks. They are attractive as a single flower, arranged together or arranged with other flowers. Like most cut flowers, they should be picked in early morning by pulling out the stems desired and recut under water. They brighten our home all summer long.

Alstroemerias like well-drained soil. They grow best in full sun, but tolerate partial shade. The height of the plant will vary depending on the amount of sun it receives and the plant cultivar. Flowering stems are shorter on plants that are grown in full sun. As most plants, they respond to compost, mulch, regular watering and fertilizer. In our garden, we don't fertilize the plants but do provide compost, mulch and regular water. They do quite well. You can encourage continuous blooming by pulling the stems for cut flowers rather than cutting them: it seems to stimulate growth. Alstroemerias store carbohydrates and water in rhizomes. This enables them to withstand a certain amount of neglect. However, their roots are brittle, making them somewhat difficult to transplant. If planted at proper depth and mulched in winter, Alstroemerias are hardy in cold weather climates.

Most plants available are sterile hybrids and are propagated from rhizomes, although some hybrids have seeds and are available from seed catalog companies. The two major seed hybrids offered by seed companies are Litgu Hybrids and Dr. Salter. They are available through several seed companies on the internet. Local nurseries I visited only carried hybrids, which are not identified by species, but identified by cultivars such as 'Watermelon,' 'Salmon,' 'Flamingo,' 'Yellow King,' 'Little Eleanor,' 'Sweet Laura,' and others.

Alstroemerias have been cultivated in Europe for over two hundred and fifty years. In 1753, Clas Alstroemer, the Swedish Consul in Spain, sent seeds of the plant to his tutor, Linnaeus, the famous botanist who developed the binomial nomenclature classification system. The seeds had just arrived in Spain from South America. Linnaeus was so impressed with the flowering plant that grew from his student's seeds, he named it *Alstroemeria pelegrina*. The introduction of *A. pelegrina* was just the beginning. Over the next two and one-half centuries, dedicated botanists gathered and sent another one hundred species to Europe from Chile and Brazil.

In the 1950s, J. Goemans of England and Maurets van Staaveren of Holland started breeding alstroemerias for the cut flower industry. They crossed *A. aurea* with several other species with excellent results. They immediately sought breeder rights for their new cultivars, which protected them from unauthorized production. As a result, alstroemerias, which had changed little over two centuries, had improved colors, larger flowers, sturdier and longer stems, and a flowering period extended from a few weeks to several months. The new cultivars were non-invasive (caution: some varieties are invasive) and more frost tolerant. This substantially increased the production of alstroemerias. Increased popularity led to further development and there is now a wide choice of my favorite flowers available to suit home gardeners' needs.

Exotic Epiphyllums:
"Orchids" of the Cactus World

~

by Virginia Havel

May to June is the season when epiphyllums are bursting with brilliant, exotic flowers, and when you discover them as I did, you may be hooked and want to grow them in your garden. The plants are easy to maintain, and are virtual "flower factories" during their blooming period. The stems and branches are also attractive in form and color, and are especially suitable for hanging arrangements.

I was first introduced to the world of epiphyllums by Paul Rice, president of the San Francisco Epiphyllum Society. I visited his growing laboratory, a lath house in Sonoma County, and was amazed to see a vast room of potted plants, stacked on shelves on all sides and hanging from the roof beams. These were plants he has collected, traded, propagated, hybridized or grafted. Each was carefully dated, identified and labeled with its genealogy, description, and horticultural name. The enthusiasm of this connoisseur was so infectious that I determined to learn more about these little-known plants.

Epiphyllums are members of the cactus family. They are often called "orchid cacti" because of their spectacular flower size and varieties of color. Unlike cacti of the dry hot desert, orchid cacti evolved in moist tropical jungles of the New World. They developed a special niche high in the tree canopy with regular rainfall, continuous warmth, dappled sunlight and sufficient air circulation. These epiphytic cacti are usually anchored in tree forks. They absorb water and nutrients from short aerial roots. Debris deposited by rain, wind and animals provide all the fertilizer necessary for their arboreal lifestyle. Only a few species of epiphyllums are terrestrial, with modified aerial roots to climb up tree trunks into the sunlight.

Epiphyllums are true cacti as recognized by the presence of areoles along the edges of notched or scalloped branches. Areoles are the pads where bristles, spines and/or flowers may arise. Lacking leaves, epiphyllums conduct photosynthesis in their flattened or triangular stems and branches. Some species have a drooping habit, suitable for hanging baskets, while others are upright. Like all other cacti, stems and branches are succulent, water storing, and modified for reduced evaporation. Unlike desert cacti, epiphyllums lack spines and have reduced bristles.

Early European explorers discovered epiphytic cacti in the jungles of Mexico, Central and South America that were pale or white, fragrant and ephemeral night-bloomers. Few epiphyllum species had exciting colors, and it took years of hybridizing these with other cacti to produce modern varieties with colorful day-blooming and longlasting flowers. There are over 13,000 species of registered hybrids in every color but blue. Flowers range in size from one- to three-inch miniatures to twelve-inch or larger giants.

Because of all the crossing of species and genera for the epiphyllum market, there is confusion about the naming of plants. The name "epiphyllum" refers to flowers that grow on the leaves. Actually, the flowers grow on the stems and branches that function as leaves. The genus *Epiphyllum* is just one of many epiphytic cacti species used in hybridizing. When epiphyllums are written with a small "e," it is including all of these genera and hybrids. The genus *Epiphyllum* was established by Adrian Haworth in 1813, who first described *Epiphyllum phyllanthus*. Scientific names are always italicized, while the hybrids are referred to as Epiphyllum Hort with the cultivar name. Most growers and collectors simply call all their plants "epis," and this nickname is accepted by the Epiphyllum Societies.

As with orchids, it is easy to produce hybrids by taking pollen from the anthers (male) of one flower and transporting it to the stigma (female) of another species. After fertilization of the ova, the developing fruit or "apple" becomes reddish as it matures and seeds ripen inside. New plants from these seeds may be surprisingly different from either parent. It takes about six years before the first flowers appear and the results are often disappointing. If a new plant turns out to be desirable, displaying new characteristics, propagation by cuttings is the sure way of getting dependable copies for the market.

Making cactus cuttings is not complicated. A piece of stem or a short branch is removed from the parent plant. Cuttings are strong, succulent and resist drying, so there is no need to rush the rooting process. Allow the cut surface to heal over by waiting until a callus forms in a couple of weeks. This will prevent the ends from rotting after planting. Apply Rootone in powdered form to the cut surface to aid in root formation. Plant in loose, moist (not soggy) potting mix, and do not water again for several weeks. Then add water regularly, but never let the cutting get soaked or dried out. It takes about a year for a new plant to reach the flowering stage. Grafting a branch of a selected cultivar onto an established plant greatly reduces the time before flowering.

Epiphyllums require the same care and conditions as the related Christmas cacti (*Schlumbergera*), but bloom at a different season. For best results, plant in light well-drained planting mix. Water and feed epiphyllums regularly with a balanced plant food. The nitrogen component is eliminated during the pre-blooming months to encourage more blossoms during April through June. They do best in filtered sunshine with high humidity. Epiphyllums thrive outdoors year-round in mild locations, and are also successful indoor plants in sunny windows. They do not have many diseases or pests. Approved safe controls may be applied when insect damage is noticed on buds and flowers.

Bamboo

~

BY BARBARA J. EUSER

Tall stems sway in the wind; sun shines through the rustling leaves, dappling the ground below. "Bamboo is an image of resilience, as is easily understood because of its supple nature…[I]ts hollow trunk metaphorically depicted the Zen principle of an empty heart (*mushin*)," according to Marc P. Keane in *Japanese Garden Design.*

Bamboo can add a feeling of grace and serenity to the garden—and an oriental tone. It can be used as a decorative element, a windbreak, or a privacy screen. It will prevent soil erosion and provide food for the table as well as forage for animals. Depending on its intended use in the garden, there are dozens of species to choose from.

But one should not plant bamboo without giving the matter sufficient thought. If you are going to grow bamboo, plan for containment! There are two main types: running and clumping. Running bamboo spreads by rhizomes that may grow two to three feet underground. These bamboos are hard to confine, even to pots. Clumping bamboos are much less aggressive. Their rhizomes tend to grow straight up instead of out, and the plant stays confined to a slow-growing clump.

Certain species of running bamboo can be extremely invasive. In genera including *Arundinaria*, *Chimonobambusa*, and *Phyllostachys*, the underground stems grow varying distances from the parent plant before sending up shoots. If they are not controlled, they may eventually produce large groves.

According to the website of the American Bamboo Society (www.americanbamboo.org): "If bamboo has been planted without root barrier and is now growing where you don't want it, you have several choices. The choices all start out with digging a trench about three feet deep around the area where you want the bamboo to grow. You can then install root barrier, pour concrete at least three inches thick or fill the trench with loose gravel. If you choose root barrier or concrete, you should leave an inch or two above ground level to make it easier to find the roots that try to escape over the top of the barrier. If you choose the loose rock fill, you will have to use a sharp spade at the beginning of every growing season to cut down into the trench and sever any new roots that try to cross the trench. Rhizomes that have already extended outside their area can be dug up. If that isn't practical, continue to knock over all new shoots you see for the next few seasons, once the rhizomes are severed from the main plant, and the rhizomes will eventually die."

If you have a large space to fill, running bamboo may be a solution. For most of us, the answer is to choose a different species of bamboo.

Clump bamboo, including *Bambusa*, *Chusquea*, *Fargesia*, and *Otatea*, have underground stems that grow only a short distance before sending up new stems. They form manageable clumps that expand slowly around the edges. To contain them completely, these bamboo may be grown in large pots or redwood boxes. Clump bamboo come in various shapes and hues. *Bambusa oldhamii* is known as the clumping giant timber bamboo and grows between fifteen and fifty-five feet tall. *Bambusa multiplex* 'Alphonse Karr' grows between eight and thirty-five feet and has culms (stems) brightly green and yellow striped. Buddha's Belly Bamboo, *B. ventricosa*, stays small when grown in containers and produces swollen culms that give it its name. Chinese Goddess Bamboo, *B. m. riviereorum*, has tiny, lacy fern-like leaves that grow on gracefully arching culms.

To propagate bamboo, dig up a clump of it, making sure to keep it moist and plant it immediately before it dries out. The best time to divide clumps for propagation is just before the growing season begins in the spring.

According to Philip Cave in *Creating Japanese Gardens*, "Bamboos generally like a moisture-retentive soil with a reasonable clay and organic matter content, although the black bamboo (*Phyllostachys nigra*) colors up best in sandy soil." Bamboo should be watered during its fast growing season in the spring. It also needs water if its leaves curl during a dry summer spell. Depending on the species, it may prefer anything from full sun to full shade. Leaves that drop can be left around the base of the plant to serve as mulch and provide the silica it will need for future growth.

Pests that attack bamboo include the bamboo mite and aphids. Gophers like to eat the shoots.

Humans also find bamboo shoots good to eat. Bamboo growers reportedly snack on them while working during the "shooting" season. Although some bamboos contain cyanogens and must be cooked before eating, this is generally not a problem with bamboos grown in temperate climates. Most can be eaten without cooking if they are not too bitter.

More than one hundred bamboo species are sold in North America. All but Japanese timber and hedge bamboo are hardy to at least 0° F.

Long-Lasting Lavender

~

BY BARBARA J. EUSER

The Spanish lavender (*Lavendula stoechas*) in my garden is just beginning to bloom. It seems a bit early this year. In fact, it may be blooming before the yellow narcissus have finished. If so, the contrast will be magnificent. Of the four species of lavender I have planted, Spanish lavender blooms first. Its flowers are dark purple, each one topped with a whirligig of intensely colored bracts. I planted a large clump of seven plants, expecting each one to grow to three feet across. So far, only two of the seven have grown that large. However, California poppies have seeded themselves in between the lavender plants. I am looking forward to a bright show in a few weeks time.

DISTRIBUTION AND CARE

Lavenders are native to the Mediterranean countries, with climates characterized by dry summers and wet winters, with moderate temperatures year-round. However, lavenders are not limited to Mediterranean climates and some varieties can survive winter snows.

Lavenders do not require much summer water, making them perfect candidates for low-water-use gardens. They do require watering the first year, but once plants are established, overwatering may kill them. Although several sources maintain that lavenders need loose, fast-draining soil, I have observed that they are growing very well in the dense clay soil of my garden. If soil is too rich, the plants will develop lovely foliage, but few flowers. The Spanish lavender in my upper garden is the champion self-seeder among my garden plants.

All my lavenders benefit from pruning after they bloom. It is safe to cut off as much as one-third of the plant. Pruning more than that is too stressful and may weaken the plant. When I don't cut my lavenders back, the old stems becomes woody, old foliage turns black and only the new growth on stem tips is green. After three or four years, the bushes (they will have become bushes in that time!) may become scraggly. Don't be afraid to replace them. In my garden, I have combined lavender with rosemary, santolina, nepeta, yarrow and verbena, which all require similar amounts of water, soil and sun.

DOMESTIC USE

Lavender's name comes from the Latin *lavare,* meaning to wash. Because of its fresh fragrance, in Roman times lavender was used in soap, and sprigs may have been added to the wash water itself. After the fall of the Roman Empire, bathing went out of fashion. In Elizabethan times, lavender perfumes were used to cloak unpleasant odors.

Lavender can also be used in cooking. Lavender leaves and flowers are used in savory dishes to flavor meats and sauces. According to herbalist Jethro Kloss, lavender flowers can be steeped in boiling water as a tonic tea which prevents fainting and allays nausea. I have a favorite recipe for lavender lemonade which calls for infusing fresh or dried lavender blooms: combine one cup of sugar with two and one-half cups of water and bring to a boil over medium heat, stirring to dissolve the sugar. Add a generous handful (about one-quarter cup) fresh lavender blooms or one tablespoon dried lavender blooms (no stems) to the sugar water, cover, and remove from heat. After it stands from twenty minutes up to several hours, strain the mixture. Add one cup of freshly squeezed lemon juice and another two and half cups of water. Stir well and serve over ice, garnished with fresh lavender sprigs.

In my garden, in addition to Spanish lavender, I have planted English lavender (*L. angustifolia*). According to one source, it is the most widely planted lavender and the classic lavender used for perfumes and sachets. I planted the dwarf variety 'Hidcote' which grows in a compact one-foot dome, then sends out long two-foot spikes with flowers at the tip. These long spikes are essential if one is making lavender wands. These pretty gifts require twenty or so spikes, a few yards of quarter-inch ribbon and a little practice to make. With the ribbon, tie the spikes together just underneath the flowers, then turn the cluster upside down. Fold back the stems and use the ribbon to weave a tight enclosure around the hidden flower heads.

I have also planted French lavender (*L. dentata*) with its distinctive tooth-edged leaves. It blooms profusely with clusters of pale purple flowers on short stems. During a past mild winter, it bloomed almost continually.

The fourth variety of lavender in my garden is a variety of *L. intermedia* called 'Provence,' grown in France commercially for use in perfume. For hundreds of years, the valleys of Provence have been filled with the color and distinctive fragrance of this lavender.

For use in sachets, I cut and dry the spent blooms of 'Provence,' French and English lavender. I have read that the correct procedure is to cut flowers from their stems just as the color begins to show, but I am unwilling to sacrifice their color and fragrance in the garden. By contrast, I have determined that the fragrance of Spanish lavender is weak and the blooms are not worth the effort to gather and dry.

I am trying to improve the overall habitat in my garden for beneficial insects and birds. My lavender plants are important in that regard. They provide nectar for bees and other insects from spring, when the Spanish lavender blooms, through English lavender in the summer and fall when 'Provence' is at its best. And if we have a mild winter, the French lavender keeps providing insect food year round.

Easy Orchids: One Inside, One Outside

~

BY KATIE MARTIN

I only grow two orchids, *Cymbidium* outside and *Phalaenopsis* inside. I have always thought that orchids have special culture requirements that I would be too lazy to fulfill. I've had friends who say they bring a beautiful specimen home and three weeks later it's dead. On the other hand, some of our Master Gardeners grow them successfully in greenhouses with light, temperature, and humidity controls. There are many species to choose from if you have a greenhouse. *Cattleyas*, *Paphiopedilums*, and *Dendrobiums* are only a few of the 300,000 species of orchids in the world. But only *Cymbidium* and *Phalaenopsis* are really easy—no greenhouse or special care necessary!

My *Phalaenopsis* (moth orchids) are in six-inch ceramic pots in my window over the kitchen sink. The window faces east, so the plants get some morning sun, but mostly just indirect light. They get some humidity from being close to the sink. I water them only once a week with water and Schultz plant food (10-15-10). (The same liquid fertilizer I use on all my houseplants.) You can use any balanced fertilizer at half strength. Don't water the crown of the plant and after watering, don't allow water to stand in the saucer. The potting material is fir bark. Sometimes air roots may grow up out of the medium, but that's okay, just leave them. *Phalaenopsis* come in many eye-popping colors. Their flowering stalk can be two feet tall with a dozen or more flowers. And the flowers last a long time, sometimes up to two months. All my friends *"ooh"* and *"ahh"* when they are blooming.

The only pest problem I've had with the plants is scale, a sucking insect with a hard protective armor. There are several methods to get rid of this varmint. You can use a hard stream of water to dislodge the insects (not very effective), spray the leaves with insecticidal soap, or use a Q-tip or toothbrush dipped in rubbing alcohol to remove the scale. I'm told that mealybugs, another sucking insect, may also attack your plants. These can be removed with the same methods used for scale.

My other success is with the orchid *Cymbidium*. I have these growing outside year-round in twelve-inch clay pots. They are mostly in sheltered spots, one under a lemon tree and others at the edge of my gazebo. I have never covered them to protect them from frost and yet they thrive. The planting mix is a special blend sold in nurseries. They tolerate being crowded in the pot, so you don't have to divide or transplant them often. This species also has many diverse colors, sizes, and shapes to choose from. The tall flowering spike will probably need to be staked. This should be done when the plant is well watered. Be careful, it's easy to snap off the whole stalk with all its buds! (I'm speaking from sad experience.) When mine are in bloom I bring them to a place of honor at my front door, so everyone who comes can see the showy flowers. I feed these with Miracle-Gro Orchid Food (26-16-12) once in a while. I admit that I don't have a regular feeding schedule and yet they thrive. These orchids are a pleasure to grow, especially because they're so easy.

Japanese Maples in Your Garden

～

BY JULIE MONSON

Every fall I am once again surprised, sometimes shocked, at the color and magnificence of Japanese maples across the urban landscape, as their leaves turn scarlet, crimson or bronze in preparation for winter. Japanese maple (*Acer palmatum—momiji* in Japanese) is a deciduous tree, growing to twenty feet high, native to the mountains of Japan. Numerous cultivars provide a banquet of choices for the home gardener, from delicate, deeply-lobed leaves on dwarf varieties to broad-fingered leaves on shapely shade trees. Many-stemmed with graceful branching structures, some have crimson leaves in spring and fall that turn green during summer. Others are shades of red all year long.

SELECTING JAPANESE MAPLES FOR YOUR GARDEN

The first step is deciding how a Japanese maple would fit into your garden design. Japanese maples prefer sunlight, but protection from dry winds; they require water, but excellent drainage. If used as a specimen, give the tree space to grow. In a corner, three medium trees, as a small, shady grove, will limit what plants you can grow under them. A dwarf, weeping maple can flow down a bank, or lean over a pond. Maples do well in containers, for a while. I had one in a large pot for fifteen years. Once planted in the garden, it quickly became an elegant tree.

Selecting for leaf color and leaf shape can be helped by doing a little homework—that is, by looking at maples in other gardens, and by visiting nurseries when maples are in leaf. Then consult a garden reference book. Select from a reliable nursery. I not only found my maples at Momiji, a Japanese maple nursery in Sebastopol, but I learned from Sachiko Umehora how to care for them.

How to Care for Your Japanese Maple

Choose a variety of Japanese maple as closely suited as possible to your garden's climate and soil. To insure good drainage, amend the soil of the planting area with compost or peat moss. Water regularly. Because maples have a large canopy of leaves, they need a fair amount of water, especially during summer months. Maples have surface roots that should not dry out. Fertilize gently once or twice a year. How much or how often depends on what else is growing under your trees, and how quickly you want your trees to grow.

Prune young trees to shape them and control their growth. In pruning Japanese maples, Umehora cuts back twigs and branches all the way to where they emerge from larger branches. I have learned that if you cut a branch halfway back there is a tendency for the tree to sprout new growth (often multiple small branches) from this point. Prune to remove center growth, to open windows through which to see the trunks. I like to leave horizontal branches where possible, as this is typical of Japanese gardens. Prune in late fall or winter, before the trees' sap begins to rise. I prune at least twice a year, to prevent too great a shock to the plant. Be sure to leave sufficient canopy to shade the trunk, which can get sunburned in summer.

Rewards in Any Season

Japanese maples are four-season trees. The graceful branching of the bare trunks in winter is clean and spare, a relief from the lushness of summer's foliage. In spring, maples produce tiny, red leaf-shoots, and then are incredibly delicate and lacy as they slowly leaf out. Summer is a bonanza of lush, shady green or upright dark red. Fall is their glory time—a few weeks of stunning color. If your trees receive afternoon sun, the resulting color is like a stained glass window.

~

CHAPTER FOUR

~

Garden Produce

The Less Strenuous Food Garden

~

BY ELIZABETH NAVAS FINLEY

A few years ago, my vegetable garden got away from me. Before I could get around to harvesting them, the green beans turned woody, the tomatoes got squishy and the lettuces bolted into towers of yellow blossoms and bitter, inedible leaves.

Not ready to give up entirely on the pleasure of home-grown edibles, I chose another strategy: replacing some of the annual vegetables with perennial crops. Like other permanent plants, perennial edibles live on from year to year, blooming and fruiting in their season, then sometimes going dormant. They are slower crops, demanding less time and attention from the gardener.

Since my food garden consists of three raised beds, the solution was to plant two boxes with perennial berries, and leave one free for annual crops, the winter sweet peas and summer bush beans that I can choose to grow or not to grow, depending on how busy the upcoming months look. For tomatoes, I grow bush varieties in large pots so the soil can be changed and the pots sterilized each year to prevent soil-borne diseases.

After three years on this program, I enjoy a food garden that's manageable: raspberries and blueberries in summer, alpine strawberries year round, and hands full of herbs. Some years there are green beans and tomatoes that fruit earlier, since the soil warms up faster in pots.

Maintenance chores are very simple: a bit of pruning and cleanup among the raspberries in late summer, and a blanket of compost and slow release fertilizer in February. The bed of strawberries, blueberries, parsley and mints gets the same compost and fertilizer treatment in late winter, along with a cleanup of dead leaves and a light trim on the blueberries. For summer, the beds are topped with shredded leaves as mulch. The parsley, a biennial, reseeds and is weeded as needed for the kitchen.

PERENNIAL VEGETABLES AND HERBS

Of course, there are many more perennial food crops than these. This time of year, nurseries have bare-root plants of globe artichokes, asparagus and rhubarb and sometimes, tubers for girasols or Jerusalem artichokes. All of these are long-lived plants (an artichoke plant will produce for five years, asparagus for ten to fifteen years) and do best when planted in soil that's been dug and loosened eighteen to twenty-four inches deep and amended with compost. Annual applications of compost and fertilizer will ensure bountiful harvests. Other than cutting off faded leaves as they go dormant, these four plants require little care and artichokes, rhubarb and girasols, with their long-stalked sunflower blooms, are decorative enough for the flower garden, as well.

The most-appreciated edibles in my yard are the herbs—a few fresh sage and rosemary leaves for a sauté, or their woody branches for tossing on the barbecue; flavorful Italian parsley and marjoram for the months when fresh basil can't be found.

Two great herbs for teas are melissa (lemon balm) and mint, in its many varieties from pineapple to orange to chocolate. Since mints are rampant growers, control them by planting in beds surrounded by paving. To grow elsewhere, plant in a five-gallon nursery container lined with landscape cloth and sunk into the soil so the rim is no higher than ground level; this technique keeps the roots from spreading.

A sunny, dry spot is perfect for sage, rosemary, oregano (Greek as well as Mexican and Italian), thyme (regular, lemon and lime) and sweet marjoram. For intense flavor, keep plants on the dry side and don't fertilize.

An area with a half-day of sun and loamy moist soil is ideal for chives and tarragon, both perennial herbs and two of the four French *fines herbes*. The other two, chervil and parsley, an annual and a biennial, will replenish themselves if allowed to go to seed.

BERRIES

Himalayan blackberries may grow wild, but less rampant cousins of the wild blackberry like olallie, logan, and marion berries are more suited to backyard culture, especially the thornless cultivars available. All cane berries need a trellis to grow on, but otherwise care is pretty simple. In fall, cut out canes that have fruited, and in spring, train new canes up on the trellis where they will fruit one year later. Top dress with compost and an organic fertilizer in late winter.

Raspberries grow as fountain-shaped shrubs four to six feet tall and need no trellising. They like a sunny spot in well-drained loamy soil. In fall and winter cut down canes that bore fruit, keep non-fruiting canes that grew the previous season (these will fruit next summer) and limit new shoots to five per plant. Top dress with compost and fertilizer in spring.

Alpine strawberries are easier to grow than regular strawberries that send out runners. The alpines take a partly shady location and form tidy mounds of evergreen leaves. Their berries are smaller and softer than commercial ones, but are intensely flavored. They are available as bare-root plants or as seeds from Shepherd's Seed Co.

Blueberries produce well, while needing only annual clipping and fertilizing. Treat these big, six-foot tall shrubs like sun-loving azaleas: plant in a sunny spot, in well-drained acid soil and mulch with pine needles or redwood duff. Plant at least two different varieties for good pollination and fruit set. It's possible to plant varieties that mature early, midseason and late for a continuous harvest. For mild climate zones, there are low-chill varieties that don't need as many hours of cold temperatures to fruit successfully.

FRUIT TREES

Many common fruit trees such as apples, plums and peaches are a gardening challenge because they require certain amounts of winter chill, have to be sprayed for insects and diseases and require specialized pruning techniques to produce a good crop. A few fruiting trees—persimmons, figs and citrus trees—are much easier on the gardener.

Of the many citrus varieties that grow in mild climates, one of the best is an Improved Meyer lemon tree. It's hardy enough for all but the coldest spots, doesn't require much pruning, no spraying and produces sweet, fragrant lemons over a long season. For other citrus varieties, see the essay "You Too Can Grow Citrus" by Virginia Havel in this chapter.

Two varieties of persimmons for home gardens are the 'Fuyu,' flattened in shape and sweet before it gets soft, and the 'Hachiya,' acorn-shaped and astringent until very soft. They both have low winter chilling needs and are self-fruiting with male and female flowers on a single tree. Both grow into large trees, sixteen to twenty feet in height. For easier access to fruit, they can be grown as espaliers on a fence or trellis and pruned once a year to maintain their size.

Figs are also low-chill fruiting trees that don't require cross-pollination. 'Black Mission' is the most reliable for home orchards, while 'White Genoa' with green skin and strawberry colored flesh is renowned for ripening in coastal gardens.

These perennial vegetables, herbs, berries and fruits are some of my favorites. With a thoughtful selection of plants, we can enjoy harvests year after year with a minimum of strain.

Tomatoes

~

BY CHARLOTTE TORGOVITSKY

It's hard to imagine a really good meal without tomatoes—and really good tomatoes are always homegrown.

The tomato plant is native to South America. It was first brought to Europe from Mexico in 1544, where it was soon adapted into the cuisine of the Italians, French and Spanish. The first seeds to reach Europe were of a yellow variety: *"Pomi d' oro"*—"apples of gold" to the Italians, and *"Pommes d' amours"*—"apples of love" to the French. Cultures from Russia to India also adapted the tomato to their cuisine.

A hundred years later, the English still grew the fruit only as a curiosity. The Americans were even slower; it was not until 1835 that the tomato was considered palatable in this country. Though it is botanically a fruit, the tomato, *Lycopersicon esculentum*, is treated as a vegetable. It is now the most popular home-grown vegetable in America.

Tomatoes belong to the family Solanaceae, which also includes many familiar and useful plants such as potatoes, eggplants, peppers and tobacco. Many of us include members of this same plant family in our ornamental gardens with nicotiana, solanum and petunias.

There are many heirloom and hybrid varieties of tomatoes available—plants of all sizes, tomatoes of all colors. Many have been bred to be disease resistant. Look for the letters behind the named variety: "F" means resistance to fusarium wilt; "V" to verticillium wilt; "N" resistance to nematodes; and "T" resistance to tobacco virus.

For an outstanding choice of tomato varieties, start from seed. Seeds germinate readily with a little bottom heat, which can be provided by a propagation mat. A grow light ensures sturdy, compact seedling growth. Plan to start seed indoors about six weeks prior to planting out in the garden. Be sure to harden off seedlings by gradually acclimatizing them to the outside environment. Tomatoes are easy to grow and very rewarding, but they do have some specific cultural needs.

Tomatoes must have six to eight hours of sunlight a day—including full sun at ten in the morning and two in the afternoon, the best, most direct light of the day. Many people like to plant their tomatoes early in the season; others say "Wait until Memorial Day." The latter makes more sense because tomato plants do not grow well until the soil is warm, and planting earlier simply exposes the plants to pathogens. Raised vegetable beds do warm up a little earlier in the season and using water wells or hot caps around each plant helps speed the process. (A water well is a series of joined, flexible plastic tubes that are filled with water to create a freestanding circular heat sink around each seedling.)

Tomatoes are heavy feeders with a deep root system, so prepare the soil well, adding lots of compost to your planting bed. Dig a generous hole, adding a little bone meal and organic all-purpose fertilizer into the bottom of the planting hole. Seedlings gain a real advantage if planted deeply, for extra roots will develop from the buried stem. Tomatoes, and their cousins the peppers, have been shown to produce bigger yields if they are planted to the depth of the first substantial set of true leaves. Simply remove the lower leaves; long-stemmed plants can be laid horizontally in the planting hole.

Water the plants deeply and often early in the growing season. Soaker hoses and drip systems are great for tomatoes, as water on the foliage causes problems. Less water, but consistent moisture, is needed when the fruit starts to ripen. This can be achieved by adding a thick layer of mulch once the soil is thoroughly warmed. Red plastic mulch is the latest craze in tomato culture, said to increase fruit set and yields. Perhaps it works: I recorded eighty-five pounds of tomatoes from one plant, using this method!

Be sure to have some kind of cages, stakes, or trellis to support the tomato plants. Staking keeps the plants more manageable and the fruit off the ground. Pruning out some of the side shoots also helps keep the plants more manageable.

Tomatoes are divided into bush and vining varieties. Bush varieties are called determinate. They grow to a specific size, then flower and set fruit all at once. Vining, or indeterminate varieties, keep growing. They set flower and fruit all season long.

There is nothing to beat the flavor of a tomato, vine-ripened, juicy and warmed by the sun. And what could be more satisfying in a home garden than this luscious fruit in abundance? Perhaps only home-made gazpacho, Indian curries, salsas, spaghetti sauces, chutneys, jams, and relishes. There is nothing more summery and festive than a plate of fresh tomatoes—red, yellow, and green!

The Fast Food Garden

~

BY ANNIE SPIEGELMAN

Many years ago, I fled my fast-paced life in Manhattan and rented a house in the Sunset district of San Francisco. This is both where and when I began gardening. After weeding the long overgrown and neglected backyard, I was determined to grow my first vegetable garden. I was still in the process of shedding my East Coast mentality, so I expected the garden to grow overnight, i.e., none of this waiting around patiently and watching the leisurely, slacker pace of Mother Nature.

On my first visit to the local nursery, the killjoy nurseryman informed me that most vegetables take many weeks or months to reach their maturation. I looked him dead in the eye knowing he was both crazy and *wrong*. I brusquely asked to speak to the manager. The manager lady repeated the same dismal rhetoric as the nurseryman. She looked me dead in the eye as if I were both crazy and *wrong*.

(O.K., perhaps I lacked the patience for gardening after all. Maybe my real motive was to impress my brand new organic gardener boyfriend, who seemed to possess a green thumb with houseplants and heirloom tomatoes.)

Finally, out of pity and a sense of duty, the manager lady practically held my hand and walked me around the vegetable six-packs recommending some fast growers well suited for novice, petulant or impatient gardeners.

Here are a few that I have had success with and that can be planted in early winter, or in early spring:

RADISHES RULE!

Radishes are easy to care for and grow in a New York minute. Most cultivars are ready to be picked in three weeks. They grow best in cool weather and need plenty of water. Seeds germinate even faster if scattered on a damp paper towel pressed into a shallow pan. When the seeds sprout, transplant them into soil well supplied with organic matter to retain moisture. Most radishes will be ready to put in your salad in seventeen to twenty-five days. Some recommended cultivars are 'Cherry Beauty,' white 'Icicle' and 'Champion.'

Better Beets

Beets make a delicious early crop to grow. Their leaves are also edible and highly nutritious. Most beets can be ready to pick in about forty-eight days from seed. They are best planted about six weeks before your last frost date. You can sow the seeds indoors in early March and set outside in April for a mid-May harvest. Plant seedlings in loose, fine soil with good moisture. Each beet seed is actually a compound seed ball with several seeds, so make sure to thin out plants. Some recommended cultivars are 'Early Wonder,' 'Early Red Ball,' and 'Little Egypt.'

Snappy Spinach

Spinach seeds can be planted directly into the garden as early in spring as the soil can be worked. The seeds will germinate in temperatures as low as 40°F. Add compost to your soil as spinach is a heavy feeder. It's best to thin them out so that spinach plants are six inches apart. Most spinach will be ready to cook up or add to your salad in forty to forty-five days. Some recommendations are 'Indian Summer' and 'Tyee.'

Lovely Lettuce

Lettuce seeds can be planted in mild winter climates from autumn through mid-spring. Plant the seeds shallowly with a thin cover of soil. Germination will occur with temperatures still in the forties. Thin seedlings to eight inches. Leaf lettuce will mature in forty to sixty days, but butterhead lettuce will need sixty to seventy days.

'Black-seeded Simpson,' which is easy to grow and is widely available, will mature in forty-five days.

Swanky Sprouts

Growing sprouts is about as easy as it gets. Even my sister Sharon, who has a fondness for plastic houseplants, can grow sprouts! Sprouts can be grown in any climate and any time of year. Alfalfa, mustard, cress and radish seeds are all great in salads or sandwiches and they are so healthy for you. You will need a one-quart jar with a screen or cheesecloth cover. Use two to three tablespoons of seeds per quart jar. (For alfalfa seeds, just use one tablespoon per jar.) Soak seeds overnight in two times their volume of water. Drain the water the next day through the screen and place the jar on its side, out of direct sunlight. Rinse and drain two to three times a day for about a week. Leaves will turn green and you can harvest your sprouts when the leaves open. They will last in your refrigerator fully covered for up to two weeks.

Other vegetables, which will grow at "high speed" as well, are Mizuna (*Brassica japonica*), Japanese mustard, Tyfon (a Chinese cabbage), turnips, peppergrass (*Lepidium sativum*), and onions.

By the way, I ended up marrying the cute organic gardener boyfriend. But eighteen years later, I admit with sorry regret that my "patience" trait is still a work in progress…but I am waiting patiently for it to surface.

Pumpkins

~

BY ELIZABETH R. PATTERSON

One morning in early October, an enormous pumpkin appeared in front of our elementary school. The children were fascinated and wandered up to touch, sit, and play on it. It was taller than some and far heavier than any of them. I learned later that it weighed close to three hundred pounds, requiring three men to move it into place from the backyard patch in which it had grown. One little boy said that it wasn't real, and I understood his disbelief. How could a vegetable grow so large? How had we come to associate it with the fall holidays of Halloween and Thanksgiving? What exactly is a pumpkin anyway?

Botanically speaking, a pumpkin is the fruit of certain members of the Cucurbitaceae family, the fruit being the mature ovary or seed-containing vessel. Other members of the vining Cucurbitaceae family include cucumbers, melons, gourds and squashes. Pumpkin varieties can belong to the *Curbita pepo* or *Curbita maxima* species.

Pumpkins are actually winter squashes, meaning that they are harvested when the rind is hard which keeps them from spoiling through the winter months. Characteristics that distinguish pumpkins from other squashes are color (orange) and shape (round), but even within these parameters there is great variation. Pumpkin varieties range in color from the ghostly white 'Lumina' to the deep red-orange 'Rouge vif D'Etampes.' There are even blue-green pumpkin varieties, such as 'Jarrahdale' and 'Queensland Blue.' The classic Halloween pumpkin, 'Connecticut Field,' is round, but as the name suggests, 'Long Island Cheese' is flattened like a cheese wheel and 'Rock Star' is a variety that is tall and upright. The best varieties for cooking are 'Small Sugar' and 'New England Pie.'

Pumpkins range in size from miniature to mammoth. Small pumpkins, such as 'Jack be Little' and 'Wee B Little' are just three inches across. The largest pumpkins, on the other hand, weigh well over one thousand pounds. In the summer of 2003, an enormous 'Atlantic Giant' variety was grown in New Hampshire by Bruce and Mary Whittier. This pumpkin weighed 1,458 pounds!

Pumpkins are thought to have originated in Mexico. They were a staple in the diet of Native Americans who grew pumpkins along with corn and beans, a trio of vegetables known as the three sisters. Pumpkin vines ran among and around the corn. Their prickly stems and leaves discouraged foraging by deer and other animals. The Indians introduced the pumpkin to the Pilgrims and it was served at early Thanksgiving celebrations. Pumpkins were adapted to an Irish tradition of carrying lights in hollowed-out turnips on All Hallows' Eve. Jack, a wily fellow caught between heaven and hell, was said to carry this type of lantern about in his wanderings. When the Irish came to America they found the pumpkin a perfect vessel for candles. The carved face of a hollowed-out pumpkin became Halloween's symbol, the jack-o'-lantern.

To have a plentiful supply of pumpkins for carving and cooking, consider planting your own pumpkin patch next spring. Pumpkins require room to grow and at least six hours of sunlight per day, but otherwise aren't too fussy. Seeds of unusual varieties can be ordered from sources such as Johnny Selected Seeds or Renee Shepherd Seeds or found at local nurseries. Fortunately for the novice, pumpkin growers are passionate, and there is a great deal of information available on how to grow them. My favorite source of information is the children's book and video, *Pumpkin Circle,* by George Levenson. *Pumpkin Circle* maps out the growth of the pumpkin from seed to plant to seed again, in a way that children can understand and appreciate. The author's website (www.pumpkincircle.com) is full of great information on pumpkins for growers of all ages. To grow really big pumpkins, pampering is required. Inspirational photos of pumpkin giants and growing advice can be found at www.pumpkinnook.com and www.howarddill.com.

Cool Season Vegetables

~

By Diane Lynch

Cool season vegetables can be planted almost all year round in foggy coastal microclimates and in fall through spring months in inland climates. Cool season vegetables include artichoke, peas, carrot, beet, parsnip, radish, turnip, asparagus, cabbage, celery, lettuce, arugula, chard, onion, spinach, broccoli, and cauliflower. They grow best when temperatures average 55° to 75°F, and will usually tolerate a bit of frost when mature. Many of these are easy to grow from seed, while some such as artichokes and asparagus are perennials, more efficiently grown from plants or roots available from a nursery.

Interestingly, the nutritional value of these cool weather crops is better than many warm season vegetables because more of the plant (roots, stems, leaves or immature flowers) is consumed; summer vegetables are usually fruits such as tomatoes, beans, corn and squash. It is also fascinating to note that, in general, the more deeply colorful the vegetable, the higher the anthocyanin level. Anthocyanins are antioxidants that are thought to protect many body systems from disease.

Chemical Free

Growing some of your own vegetables is not only healthy because what you harvest is at the peak of freshness, but because you can control what chemicals you ingest by using organic or less toxic methods. General rules for minimizing the use of poisons include:

- careful monitoring of the garden to check for signs of pests or damage
- selecting resistant varieties, such as lettuce resistant to downy mildew

* using mechanical methods to prevent insect damage, like row covers to keep flea beetles from dining on the arugula, going on snail hunts at night, spraying aphids off with a blast of water which breaks off their mouthparts and renders them unable to feed
* disposing of infected/infested foliage promptly to prevent the spread of disease
* rotating crops, alternating plant families in a given space
* promoting beneficial insects as natural biological controls

A Growing Example

Rosalind Creasy grows an astounding array of unusual vegetables (as well as chickens in a vine-covered coop) in the sunny front yard of her small suburban lot in Los Altos. She cooks with the vegetables as she develops recipes for her many cookbooks, which feature these unique varieties. Her book, *The Complete Book of Edible Landscaping,* is an encyclopedia of practically anything one might grow to eat and features extensive sections on landscape design, as well as chapters that explain and promote organic, sustainable growing techniques. This author practices what she preaches.

Part of the Landscape

Consider working some vegetables into the sunny parts of your landscape. If you are careful about planting times, you can get three crops a year from the same space: an early spring crop of greens or vegetables, followed by summer tomatoes and beans, followed by fall vegetables. Many vegetables lend themselves to trellising which adds visual interest, as well as increases the productive space in the garden. Vegetables can be a beautiful part of the landscape: imagine teepees of peas or beans and borders of lettuce in red, green and shades in-between. A walk through the seed aisles in a garden center could inspire you to try some new plants in your garden, as well as add some interesting new foods to your diet.

Enjoying Herbs Year Round

~

BY SALLY LUCAS

I grew up in the English countryside and my father grew just two herb varieties: parsley, which my mother used in a white sauce to be served with fish, and mint (which he tried to control rather than grow) used to flavor new potatoes.

Herbs can be a rewarding crop whether you grow them on a sunny windowsill in your city apartment or in the expanse of a large country garden. They are relatively easy to grow and require minimum care. Annual plants which generally die in the same year that you plant them (for example, basil, dill, and cilantro) can be grown from seed in the spring and perennial plants which last for several years (for example, thyme, mint, chives, and rosemary) can be started by seed, cuttings or division, also in spring.

By summer, your plants should be producing enough for your kitchen use and some to spare, unless, of course, the aphids ate more than their share, as with my basil this year! Pick fresh herbs from the top of the plant and gather a few leaves at a time as you need them. This will encourage the plant to produce more growth and become bushy. Keep the leaves cool and dry until you use them and do not chop them until ready to add to your dishes, or they will begin to lose their aroma and flavor.

If you do have an abundant supply, preserving now will allow you to surround yourself with herbal products throughout the fall and winter months. Whether you make herbal tea, potpourri, or use dried herbs in your cooking, there is a special satisfaction in knowing you grew the herbs yourself.

There are several ways to preserve your harvest. Freezing or preserving in oil or vinegar are the best ways, but many gardeners prefer drying because it is so easy.

The best time to pick herbs for drying is just before they bloom; leaf production declines after flowering. Cut six inches below the flower buds in the late morning, after the leaves have dried out and before the hot sun draws out the flavor and aroma. Up to 75 percent of the current season's growth can be harvested at one time. Harvesting in early summer will allow for plenty of new growth for many more harvests. Annual herbs can be harvested until frost; perennial herbs can be clipped until one month before the first frost. Remove any dead or damaged leaves and wash gently in cold water, drying on paper towels. Don't pick stems for drying that you wouldn't use fresh—their properties will not improve on drying and the results will be disappointing. Make bunches about one inch in diameter, wrapping the stems with a small rubber band. Label them and hang them upside down out of direct sunlight. Drying time will vary and is dependent on humidity, temperature and the type of herb. Test after three days: if a leaf crumbles easily between your fingers, it is probably ready. This process may take up to fourteen days. Remove the leaves from the stems and seal in glass jars for a week. If moisture has condensed on the inside of the glass, remove the contents, spread out and continue to dry. Store in a glass jar that is kept in the dark for up to one year.

Herbs (especially parsley) can also be successfully dried between layers of paper towels in the microwave, but this process requires careful attention as the paper towels can catch fire. Run the microwave on high for two minutes and then check for dryness. If they are not done, continue for a further thirty seconds and check again. Do not leave the microwave unattended.

Conventional ovens can also be used to dry herbs. Spread the herbs on cookie sheets and dry at the lowest temperature setting possible. Home food dehydrators also do an excellent job of drying herbs. Follow the directions provided with the dehydrator.

Some herbs, including chives, tarragon and dill, freeze very well. Rinse and dry the leaves (some herbs with small leaves freeze best if left on the stem) and lay them out on a baking tray in the freezer. Pack tightly in a freezer bag and use as required. Diced herbs can be frozen in an ice cube tray, covered with water or stock and used in soups and stocks. Herb blends can be mixed: try equal quantities of thyme, basil, sage, sweet marjoram, and crushed fennel seeds for fish. For poultry, try equal amounts of sweet marjoram, basil, thyme, and lemon thyme.

My own container garden includes more than ten different varieties of herbs that I use in Indian, Italian, Spanish, and Greek dishes. What new varieties will you be tempted to grow next year?

Growing Garlic, aka The Stinking Rose

~

BY DIANE LYNCH

Looking for a vegetable the deer won't eat, which requires little water, takes little space, and will last most of the year? Try growing some garlic. There are about one hundred varieties of garlic in cultivation around the world and folks who know these things say that there are significant differences in taste among them. Garlic is either classified as softneck (*Allium sativum*) or hardneck (*A. sativum* var. *ophioscorodon*). Another species, elephant garlic, *A. ameloprasum*, is enormous, but lacks any genuine garlic flavor and is actually a leek. Softneck garlic is generally milder in flavor and keeps longer—this is what you will find in the grocery store. Hardnecks have more intense flavor, a hard stalk up the middle, and don't store quite as well, but they are thin-skinned and usually very easy to peel. Within these categories there are dozens of varieties.

Garlic is typically planted in the fall in a mild winter climate, mid-October to late November. It can also be planted in the spring, but fall is best because the colder temperatures of winter stimulate the formation of the cloves. Try local farmers' markets or nurseries for unusual varieties. Break the bulbs apart into cloves and select only the largest cloves to plant, using the others for cooking. Deep, well-drained soil is best for growing garlic and some growers advocate raised beds, which can be very deep and are easy to work. Bone meal is a good fertilizer to work in at planting time as it will supply ample phosphorus for good bulb development, or use a complete 5-10-10 fertilizer. Plant cloves root or flat end (the part that is attached to the base of the bulb) down, three to six inches apart and twice their length deep, in rows a foot or so apart.

Water regularly but don't over-soak your garlic, as it doesn't like wet feet. Keep it weeded since weeds rob the soil of nutrition and

98

water that should be going to your crop. Mulching with wheat or rice straw (other types, as well as hay, have too many weed seeds) or other organic matter makes weeding a breeze. In six weeks or so you'll see the green blades coming up and by this time the winter rains should have taken over your watering responsibilities for a while. In April, give your crop two foliar feedings of fish emulsion and Maxicrop or other mineral supplement—mix in a watering can and sprinkle on or put through a sprayer. In May or June the tips will begin to turn brown—continue watering for another couple of weeks, then stop watering to allow the bulbs to dry out as the tops die down.

Hardneck garlic will sometimes develop a flowering stem called a scape, which if left to grow will form a tiny garlic bulbil. This is usually not fertile and most people remove them as soon as they appear so the plant's energy continues to be put to bulb formation. Scapes can be used in salads or sautéed with other vegetables.

By midsummer when the tops are at least half brown or yellow or have fallen over, it is time to dig up the garlic. Use a fork or shovel to dig, instead of pulling the bulbs up. Pulling can crack the stalk, greatly shortening storage time. Leaving the tops on, hang the garlic in a shady place with good air circulation for about three weeks. By this time it should be dry and you can trim the roots and tops off (leave about an inch) and store it in the pantry in ventilated clay pots or baskets. Alternatively, you can braid the softneck varieties before hanging or allow them to dry and re-wet the tops to braid after thoroughly dry.

Some of the varieties that do well in the San Francisco Bay Area and other mild climates include the hardnecks 'Rocambole,' 'Purple Stripe' and 'Porcelain' and the softnecks 'California Early,' 'California Late' and 'New York White.' Check with your supplier to see which do best in your microclimate because some, such as 'California Early' and 'California Late,' need about six weeks of temperatures around 40°F to do well, and some don't do well in warmer areas. But don't let these technicalities keep you from experimenting with garlic. It can be very tolerant and you don't need a blue ribbon at the county fair to produce enough to keep you cooking with garlic all year—along with the satisfaction of having grown it yourself.

Sonoma farmer Chester Aaron grows ninety-four varieties of garlic from thirty countries on his picturesque small farm in Occidental, California. He uses raised beds about two feet tall wired at the bottom to foil the gophers, although they usually don't particularly favor garlic. He supplies people all over the United States with his garlic, as well as some of the toniest restaurants on the West Coast. And he's a font of fascinating information about the health benefits and lore of garlic, which he has set forth in a series of books such as *The Great Garlic Book* and *Garlic is Life*.

Filaree Farm in Washington state is a supplier of unusual and mundane garlics and they will help you pick varieties that will do well in your area. Their website (www.filareefarm.com) has very good descriptions of the garlics, and they sell books about garlic as well. Get ready to grow some garlic this fall!

Savoring the Harvest

~

BY MAGGIE AGRO

You've planted well and harvest has been abundant, but now it's the end of the season, the weather is getting cooler and you have a load of leftovers from the garden. You don't have the time or the inclination for canning, and your friends and neighbors just don't want any more. There are quick and easy alternatives, but start with proper handling for longest life.

To get the most out of your fruits and vegetables, harvest them in the early morning, just after the dew has dried. This catches them at their very freshest with an extra crispness of texture imparted by cool night temperatures. Never leave them out in the sun where they can dehydrate very quickly. Immediately use any bruised or soft vegetables.

To buy extra time until you can deal with them, store them properly and you can add days to their fresh life. Brush dirt off vegetables to be stored and, if necessary, wash lightly and dry thoroughly before storing.

REFRIGERATION

Do not put ripe fruits together with vegetables in the crisper. Many ripe fruits produce ethylene gas, which causes yellowing of green vegetables, sprouting of potatoes, russet spotting of lettuce, toughening of asparagus, and bitter taste in carrots. Cole crops (for example, cabbage and broccoli) give off strong odors that may be absorbed by other foods in the refrigerator. Eggplant, okra, potatoes (protect from light to prevent greening), hard rind squashes and pumpkins and ripe tomatoes may be stored in a basement or a cool, dark part of a garage. Bell peppers, cucumbers, ripe melons, snap beans, and summer squash need cooler temperatures (45° to 55°F), but cannot take the chill of the refrigerator longer than five days.

Chard, escarole, endive, collards, green onions, lettuce, spinach, and most leafy greens should be washed and drained well and stored in the refrigerator crisper that is more than half full to keep humidity high. Asparagus, beets, broccoli, cabbage, carrots, peas, radishes, and unhusked sweet corn should be stored in a separate crisper or in plastic bags in the main compartment of the refrigerator.

Freezing

Prepare vegetables for freezing by blanching them in boiling water for recommended times. The County Extension office has information on specific times for various foods. Blanching vegetables is absolutely necessary to inactivate enzymes that cause undesirable changes in flavor and texture. It also reduces the number of microorganisms on the food and enhances the color.

Herbs

Herbs can be kept in a glass of water covered with a plastic bag for immediate use. To dry, hang small-leafed herbs in bunches in a warm, dry, well-ventilated area for three to ten days. Larger leaves can be spread on newspapers to dry or gently heated in an oven with an open door. Leaves are sufficiently dry if they crackle when touched. Store out of sunlight and heat. Should any sign of moisture reappear, just redry.

To dry herbs in the microwave, rinse and dry herbs well. Remove leaves from stems and microwave leaves, one layer at a time, on paper towels for three minutes at high power or until they feel dry and crackle to the touch. Do not leave the microwave unattended. Thin-leafed herbs work best. You can chop them by pulsing them in a clean coffee mill. Store in an airtight jar. Clean the mill by chopping bread cubes and wiping out with a towel. Unplug before cleaning.

To freeze, wash, pat off excess water, place in plastic bags and put into the freezer immediately. Or put chopped herbs into an ice cube tray, fill with water and freeze. Put the cubes into plastic bags and store in the freezer. Cubes can easily be popped into soups, stews or sauces.

TOMATOES

At the end of the season, you can pull up your entire tomato plant with green-ripe (straw-colored) tomatoes and hang the plant by the stem in the garage for mature fruit to ripen. Be sure to place something soft beneath the plant to catch tomatoes as they ripen and fall from the vine.

Tomatoes which have been scalded for thirty seconds in boiling water may be frozen raw and whole. Select especially meaty ones for freezing and place the whole or sliced blanched tomatoes on a greased cookie sheet in the freezer for twenty-four hours. When frozen solid, put them into containers.

LAST RESORTS

If all else fails, you can always make zucchini bread and tomato sauce to freeze for a chilly day in winter. And there are specialty items like the antipasto caponata (a spicy Italian vegetable mixture that freezes well) that is great on rounds of toast. Finally, don't forget to compost damaged vegetables and plants at the end of the season.

Good Enough to Eat:
Safe and Tasty Flowers

~

BY ANNIE SPIEGELMAN

Every once in a while I become possessed by the spirit to create a homegrown organic meal for my husband and young son. I make a dazzling presentation of elegant plate settings and entrees garnished with flower blossoms, all served by me, the happy hostess. This throws the two of them off, at least temporarily. They go to sleep that night with satisfied smiles on their sweet innocent faces. They imagine me as a good mother and flawless wife in startling contrast to the egocentric, opinionated, cranky hack they're used to living with on a daily basis.

On those special, albeit rare, occasions, I make sure to use flowers from our garden for both ornamental and culinary purposes. Cooking with flowers is an ancient tradition traced back to Roman times. The practice continued on strongly through the Victorian era when flowers from the garden, notably roses and orange blossoms, were used quite often. Cookbooks from that time offer recipes for salads and soups that include violet flowers, marigold, primrose, rosehips and strawberry leaves.

There are a few safety guidelines for adding flowers to your food. Use only clean garden flowers that you know have not been sprayed. Use flowers that you know are edible. If you have any question, call your local poison control center.

Below are some edible flowers that are widely recognized as safe to ingest. It is advised to use small amounts initially in the event of a potential allergy.

NASTURTIUM (*Tropaeolum majus*)

We are fortunate that nasturtiums grow in our yard almost as easily as a weed. We love nasturtiums and use them in salads, sandwiches and soups. The round-shaped leaves as well as the brilliant sunset-colored blossoms are edible and have a wonderful peppery taste similar to watercress. Nasturtiums grow best in poor soil and can tolerate neglect, making it a great flower to grow for novice gardeners or children. Nasturtiums are annuals and grow best in full sun. In general, the poorer the soil the more flowers one can expect. I'm telling you, this plant is win-win! There are a variety of cultivars which all grow easily from seed: dwarf, tall, or climbing from one to three feet.

BORAGE (*Borago officinalis*)

I planted a few borage seeds about three years ago and now every spring we have large areas spreading like a ground cover around our yard. The delicate star-shaped flowers are a beautiful, hypnotizing sky blue. The blossoms are sweet and small like forget-me-nots and have a cool, cucumber taste. Borage blossoms can be used to garnish lemonade, sorbet or a gin and tonic! In the summer, children will enjoy freezing them in an ice tray. The leaves are also good in a salad, but need to be finely chopped to reduce their furry texture. The borage plant is high in calcium, potassium and mineral salts. Borage can easily be grown from seed. Plants do best in full sun but ours grow equally well in light shade. Borage will self-sow for years to come. Folks, it doesn't get any easier than this.

CALENDULA (*Calendula officinalis*)

Calendula, or pot marigold, was used in medieval times to effectively treat a variety of ailments. It is still often found as an ingredient in skin lotions. The yellow or orange petals can easily be plucked from the flower head, discarding the rest. A fresh handful of calendula petals looks nice tossed onto a salad of mixed greens. Dried petals can be stirred into chowders, muffin mixes or paella, as a homegrown colorful and sharp substitute for saffron. Calendula grows to eighteen inches and does exceptionally well in full sun. They look best in the early summer and then get a bit straggly during the hotter days of August. Cut back after first bloom to encourage new growth in the fall.

ALLIUM (LEEKS, CHIVES, GARLIC)

Known as the "flowering onions," there are approximately four hundred species that includes onions, garlic, chives, and shallots. Alliums have marvelous health properties and a long tradition of both medicinal and culinary use. All members of this genus are edible and all parts of the plant are edible. The flowers have a stronger flavor than the leaves and the young seed-heads are even stronger. The leaves and flowers can be added to a salad. The leaves can also be cooked in soups and stews. Seeds, bulbs or nursery plants can be planted in mild winter climates in autumn in rich, well-drained soil in a sunny location.

Some other safe and tasty edible flowers you can grow are: bee balm (*Monarda*), squash, forget-me-nots, lavender, roses, Johnny-jump-ups (*Viola*), fennel, carnations, *Angelica* and dandelions.

Asparagus

~

BY ELIZABETH R. PATTERSON

The appearance of locally grown asparagus in the market is a true sign of spring. This delicacy, cultivated by the Romans two thousand years ago, is the newly emerging shoot of the plant *Asparagus officinalis*. If left to grow, the sprouts of this perennial vegetable become lush, feathery ferns. One way to assure a steady supply of sweet, fresh asparagus is to grow your own. While establishing an asparagus bed takes forethought and patience, the initial effort will be well rewarded with ten to fifteen years of harvests.

First, carefully select a site in the garden that receives full sun and can be devoted to the production of asparagus. Then eliminate perennial weeds and amend the soil prior to planting the bed. Asparagus requires neutral, well-drained soil that is loose and light and full of well-composted organic matter. In preparation for planting, dig in plenty of fertilizer (about twenty pounds of 10-20-10 fertilizer per 1,000 square feet). Once asparagus has been planted, digging in the bed will damage roots and limit production.

The size of the asparagus bed will depend on the number of eaters. With twenty plants, our garden supplies five family members with a weekly meal of asparagus during harvest. For more enthusiastic eaters, plan on ten plants per person. Unfortunately, each asparagus plant requires approximately five square feet of space, which means a bed of one hundred square feet will be necessary to accommodate twenty plants. A long row of asparagus can be planted along a fence or at the edge of a vegetable bed.

Asparagus can be planted from seed or crowns, the dormant rootstock of year-old plants that look like fat, tan spiders with too many legs. Crowns are easier to plant and tend, and may take less time to get established. Look for healthy crowns at local nurseries or mail order sources. 'Martha Washington' and 'Jersey Giant' are two common varieties. Order the "all-male" variety, meaning that plants do not produce seed and are more prolific at harvest time.

Depending on your locale, crowns should be planted in late winter or spring. Dig a trough twelve inches deep in the amended, weed-free bed. Crowns should be spaced twelve to eighteen inches apart. Spread the roots of the crown over the soil and gently cover with one to two inches of soil. Do not tamp the soil down around the crowns. As the asparagus grows, add soil to the trough so that, eventually, the trough is filled in. Although asparagus is drought tolerant, the new crowns should be well watered and the plot kept free of weeds. Asparagus seeks water deep in the soil, so water deeply but infrequently later in the spring and summer.

This is where patience is needed. Do not harvest any of your asparagus the first year. Allow the ferns to develop and do not cut them back until they die back in the fall or are killed by frost. The second season, harvest early asparagus spears, but stop after two to three weeks and allow ferns to form. In following years, the harvest can be extended to six or eight weeks, beginning when shoots appear in February or March and ending when a majority of the shoots are smaller in diameter than a pencil. Harvest spears with tightly formed tips when they are approximately eight inches high by snapping or cutting them off at the base.

After harvest, feed asparagus with a source of nitrogen and water every seven to ten days. Mulching the bed will help conserve moisture and keep weeds at bay. Watering should be stopped in September to allow the plants to go dormant. Once ferns become dry they should be cut and removed from the bed to discourage the development of insect pests. Asparagus is attacked by fusarium wilt and rust. Watch for army worms, cutworms that feed on emerging tender tips in the night. Companion plants for asparagus are parsley, basil, and tomatoes, and including these plants alongside and underneath asparagus ferns will increase the productivity of the bed.

So why devote the space and time to grow asparagus? Once established, an asparagus bed requires less work than most vegetables. Asparagus is a vegetable for which freshness counts: fresh-picked asparagus is far sweeter than any you will ever find in a grocery store. And most importantly, the purplish heads of the emerging asparagus will herald the arrival of spring.

Olives

~

BY CHARLOTTE TORGOVITSKY

The best feature of the garden at our new house was the olive tree. It looked nicely established, though in need of a thorough pruning. Everything else in the garden had to go. We removed every bit of lawn and built berms and raised beds, rich with compost. Gravel pathways provided access to the planting areas.

The olive tree introduced us to our new neighbor. The olives produced by this tree, we soon learned, were bigger, plumper, and more prolific than most. Our neighbor had been picking and curing olives for several years, and wanted to continue harvesting from our tree, an arrangement he had had with the previous owners.

Our neighbor was generous with samples of his cured olives and, for a couple of years, came to pick the olives when they reached the black ripe stage in late November or December. When he tired of it, he was happy enough to share his recipe. I did a little more research and some experimenting with various methods for producing tasty table olives at home. My recipes are below.

OLIVE FRUIT FLY

In 2003, family and friends were looking forward to my olives, so I was prepared to make a real production of it. A prolific crop was developing, but a closer inspection was in order. It seemed to me that the olives were ripening much too early in the season. The fruits looked malformed, pitted, and misshapen instead of smooth and plump.

I could see little round scars on the skin. When I opened one up, grub-like larvae were evident inside. I picked a few more fruits and took them to the Master Gardener's desk in Novato, California for an

110

expert opinion. The news was not good: my olive tree, as many more throughout the state, was infested by the olive fruit fly.

Our cultivated olives, *Olea europaea*, are native to the Mediterranean region. This pest, which is host specific, also comes from that area, where it is kept in check by natural predators. The olive fruit fly first arrived in Los Angeles, apparently via Mexico, in October of 1998. Within a year, it had spread to the rest of southern California, then up through the Central Valley, and to the San Francisco Bay Area by 2002.

My olives were a total loss that year, and I noticed many more trees that were also infested. The California Department of Food and Agriculture conducted experiments with a parasitic wasp, imported from Tunisia, for biological control, as well as certain nematodes for control of pupae wintering over in the soil. In the Mediterranean region, resistant varieties of olive trees are planted and the trees are heavily pruned to let in light and air, which discourages the fly.

This fruit fly is totally dependent on the olive throughout its life cycle and the species can have several reproductive cycles in a single year. It emerges in early spring from unpicked or dropped fruit as a winged adult. When the new olive crop reaches a stage where the pit begins to harden, it gives off chemicals that trigger the development of eggs in the female fly. The female lays her eggs in the fruit, leaving an ovipositor scar, often the first sign of an infestation. The eggs hatch quickly, and the larvae tunnel throughout the fruit, destroying the pulp. The larvae pupate in the fruit, except the last generation of the year, which may leave the fallen fruits to pupate in the soil.

Preventative measures can help ensure a crop for the following year. The first step is a thorough removal and disposal of all fruits, both those remaining on the tree as well as all fallen fruits. A thorough pruning that lets light and air into the center of the tree also helps to discourage the fruit fly. A good rule of thumb is to prune so that a bird could fly through the tree.

Since it is difficult to be certain that every last infected fruit has been disposed of, hanging yellow sticky traps is a good insurance policy. Four to six traps hung throughout the tree, distributing them high and low towards the outside of the canopy and favoring the southern exposure will capture most emerging flies. There may be some beneficial insects captured this way, but it is a minimal risk.

It is doubtful that this pest can be totally eliminated, but conscientious gardeners can help reduce the infestation. Commercial growers are working with effective organic control methods, but these are not yet registered for use by the homeowner. Detailed information on more complicated control methods such as baited bottle traps and pheromone traps is available at your local Master Gardener's desk.

HOME-CURING TABLE OLIVES

It's fun and easy to produce really tasty table olives at home. I enjoy making them and my friends and family enjoy eating them! Here are a couple of simple methods for home curing table olives.

Olives can be salt or brine cured to remove the bitterness; the first method takes about a week to ten days; brine curing takes about six weeks. For both methods, black ripe olives should be picked, cleaned, and rinsed.

For salt curing: Put the olives in a plastic colander with a dish underneath, and simply sprinkle table salt generously over the olives, stirring them as you do, both morning and evening. This leaches out the bitterness; you will need to taste them to determine when to stop the process. When the bitterness has been removed, soak them one day in fresh water to reduce some of the saltiness.

For brine curing: Make a brine that is one-quarter cup of table salt to one quart of water. Each olive needs to be slit with a small sharp knife. I use a glass gallon jar, with another smaller jar filled with pie weights in the opening to keep all the olives submerged in the brine. The brine needs to be refreshed once a week, and again, taste the olives to determine when to stop the process. The olives will look pale, but the dark color is regained when the whole process has been completed.

Once the bitterness has been removed, the olives can be marinated. Use olive oil, but have some fun experimenting with various flavorings, and combinations. Some possible herbs and spices are: garlic, bay leaves, whole cayenne peppers, peppercorns, thyme, oregano, and cumin seeds. Slices of lemon or orange add an additional dimension of flavor.

Let the olives marinate for about a week, then drain off the marinade, reserving some for later use, and place the olives on a baking tray with sides. Dry them in a 250°F oven for a total of about ten hours, over the course of a few days. I usually place them in the warm oven for a couple of hours at a time, then stir them about, prick them a little, and brush them with more marinade. The oven is turned off, but I leave the olives in the warm oven. Taste them at intervals, so that you are sure not to overdry them.

After several days they are dark and shriveled and delicious! Purchase inexpensive small plastic containers for the cured olives from a restaurant supply store and refrigerate the cured olives for later use.

You Too Can Grow Citrus

~

BY VIRGINIA HAVEL

The citrus family (Rutaceae) originated in the Malay-East Indonesian Archipelago over twenty million years ago. Citrus varieties were introduced to the New World by Christopher Columbus, and now are found in all subtropical climates of the world. Some of our most widely used and delicious citrus fruits include lemons, limes, oranges, tangerines and grapefruits. Other members, kumquats, sour-acid mandarin, and rangpur limes, are often grown as ornamentals. There are numerous hybrids and cultivars of all of the above, providing tremendous choice for the home gardener.

Citrus fruits are known for their tangy flavor and piquant aroma. There is nothing quite like the delicate fragrance of orange blossoms in the garden on a sunny spring day, and what a delight it is to enhance a refreshing drink with your own fresh lemon or lime! The evergreen shiny dark foliage and bright showy fruits are attractive ornamentals on patios and in containers. Almost anyone can grow some kind of citrus, but it is necessary to select the one that suits the garden environment and microclimate.

In areas that frequently experience winter frost, many kinds of citrus can survive if temperatures do not dip below 20°F. Protection from wind by planting against a wall or house, mulching or covering roots with black weed-block cloth, and augmenting the ambient temperature with reflected sunlight from light-colored backgrounds can increase success. Equally important is the requirement for sufficient heat during the period of fruit development. Some citrus will not flower or set fruit if temperatures do not reach a required high. Southern exposure is most important to provide at least six hours of daily sun.

Good drainage is a required soil condition. Clay soil needs to be amended with compost, peat moss or bark. Planting in a mound above ground level or on a slope will improve drainage. Increasing aeration of clay soil by lifting soil slightly around plants with a pitchfork every second year after spring rains can be helpful. Granitic soil drains so rapidly that water and nutrients need to be replaced more frequently. Covering soil with mulch or compost provides some nutrients and improves water-holding capacity. Specialized citrus fertilizer (containing balanced nitrogen (N), phosphorus (P), potassium (K), iron and zinc) should be applied. Usually, twice a year is sufficient.

Proper watering of citrus is most important, as fungal diseases are common when the soil is allowed to become soggy. Water established trees no more than every two weeks in clay soil. Newly planted trees need watering twice a week on the root balls for the first two or three months after planting. Overwatering encourages various fungi such as blue or green mold and brown rot to attack plant fruits. A Phytophthora species produces a disease (gummosis) on the base of the trunk at ground level, and is particularly common in limes and lemons. Armillaria root rot occurs underground and is recognized by mushrooms in clumps around the tree's base. There is no effective treatment once it infects the plant. Avoid overhead watering or watering directly on flowers and leaves. Irrigate early in the day, allowing foliage to dry before dark.

Citrus plants are relatively disease-resistant, but can be attacked by common garden pests. Scales, aphids, whiteflies, and mealybugs are usually controlled by natural enemies. Citrus cutworms (brown to green caterpillars with white stripes on the sides) feed on blossoms and very young fruits. *Bacillus thuringiensis*, a natural biological control organism, is effective. Red citrus mites that feed on young leaves can be a problem. When natural enemies fail to keep pests in check, spray with horticultural oil between August and September. Another mite, the citrus bud mite, can deform fruits in summer and fall, particularly in coastal areas. Slugs and snails often damage leaves and fruits when limbs trail on the ground. Prune lower branches to limit entry.

Dwarf varieties grown in containers have the advantage of being moveable during periods of frost. In smaller gardens, dwarf plants can provide abundant fruit and do not need much space.

Many dwarf citrus have been developed to grow in cooler climates, requiring less heat to develop sweet fruits:

- Variegated Pink Lemon: A variety of Eureka lemon with a pinkish tinge on new leaf growth. The juicy fruit is bright yellow on the outside with pink flesh (often called "lemonade tree"). Grows to twelve to fifteen feet and fruits all year. Does well in containers and requires full sun.
- Improved Meyer Lemon: Hardy, excellent flavor, thin-skinned and juicy. A thornless, small to medium tree with year-round fruits.
- Robertson Navel Orange: Slow growth, to six to ten feet and excellent for containers. Fruits from December to April and bears fruit at a young age. The showy fruit clusters are decorative, seedless and easy to peel.
- Tavares Limequat: Hybrid of a Mexican lime and a kumquat. It tolerates cold and needs less heat than parent lines. Fruit is elongated and is mature from fall to spring.
- Oro Blanco Grapefruit: Dwarf of eight to twelve feet. A white seedless fruit able to ripen in low summer heat of coastal areas.

Persimmons: Fruit of the Gods

~

BY MARIE NARLOCK

It may be hard to imagine during these cool springtime days, but intense summer sunshine is right around the corner. If you're considering adding a shade tree to your garden to cool things off in August, then perhaps you should consider the lovely persimmon tree.

The persimmon, a deciduous tree that grows twenty-five feet tall and wide, offers distinctive year-round pleasure. In spring, its lime-green new growth sprouts quickly and consistently. Come summer, its ovate leaves have become leathery, darker green, and up to four inches wide by seven inches long, providing deep, welcoming shade and an almost tropical appearance. By autumn, the leaves have turned brilliant crimson, orange, and yellow, and provide the proverbial *crunch-crunch-crunch* underfoot. Finally, in the depth of winter, the persimmon tree is almost a comical sight, with shiny orange baseballs dangling from leafless branches—a cheery contrast to a gray December day.

And besides, how could a fruit tree possibly be bad whose genus, *Diospyros*, means "fruit of the gods"?

In addition to its striking seasonal attributes, the persimmon fruit is a healthy addition to any diet, boasting a high potassium content and more fiber, minerals, and phenolic compounds than an apple. It is also a mecca for over thirty species of birds. And the next time you're out on the golf course, remember that the wood you're swinging is most likely persimmon. Ditto the fancy inlay work on your jewelry box.

But, you may be thinking, what about all that squishy fruit?

True, persimmons are an acquired taste, often falling into the black or white categories of "I love them" or "I hate them." As

Pocahontas' Captain John Smith reported back to the English, "...the fruit is like a medlar, it is first green, then yellow, and red when ripe. If it not be ripe, it will draw a man's mouth awire with much torment. But when it is ripe, it is as delicious as an apricot."

Even if you don't think the gelatinous fruit is as delicious as an apricot, you may be surprised by the number of cake, cookie, ice cream, bread, and pie recipes in which to use your prized, and usually prolific, fruit as a healthy and unique sugar alternative. Then again, if cooking with persimmons isn't your thing, you can always simply place them in a decorative bowl inside where they make beautiful, colorful autumnal displays.

Native to China thousands of years ago and then introduced to Japan, the persimmon has become Japan's national fruit and one of the traditional foods of the Japanese New Year. The first persimmon cultivar arrived in California in the mid-1800s, making it one of the earliest commercially grown fruits in the United States.

There are many varieties of persimmons, but *Diospyros kaki* 'Hachiya' dominates, with about 90 percent of the commercial market in the United States. It is an astringent fruit, shaped like a large, pointy-bottomed tomato. Again, the key to enjoying your persimmon is to wait until it is fully ripe, whether right off the tree (if you can beat the birds) or having sat in a bowl for a while inside. Fully ripe means waiting until it is mushy, bright orange, and jelly-like inside.

The 'Fuyu' persimmon has gained in popularity in the past few years. This is probably because it is eaten when firm, crunchy, and sweet, just like an apple, shiny skin and all. It looks different than a 'Hachiya,' sort of like a smooth mini-pumpkin, flat and squat.

Persimmon flowers are inconspicuous, usually appearing in groups of one to five per twig as the new growth appears, typically through March. Temperate climates are perfect for these trees, and they have a low chilling requirement (less than one hundred hours), so they are reliable fruiters. They will tolerate partial shade, are not picky about soil, require little fertilizer, and are also somewhat drought tolerant, although the fruit will be larger and tastier with regular irrigation.

Life feels pretty good when you're reading a good book in the shade of a persimmon tree. However, during gusty afternoons, watch for brittle branches: strong winds may snap off a few, especially if they're heavily laden with fruit. Even on non-windy days, watch for swinging children! The first day that we moved into our house a sweet six-year-old decided to try out one of the branches on our "new tree" and ended up with the branch in her hands. That was my first clue that this tree would be off limits for climbing and swinging.

These trees are relatively problem free, although squirrels, deer, coyotes, rats, opossums, and birds are fond of the fruit and gophers will go after the roots. Nice if you want wildlife. Not nice if you want persimmon bread.

Jujube Dates

~

BY BARBARA J. EUSER

When I think of dates, I think of date palms in the desert. However, the red dates, black dates and honey dates found in local Oriental markets are not the fruit of palms, but of jujube trees, *Ziziphus jujuba*. With their deep roots, jujube trees tolerate desert conditions and are worthy of consideration for drought-tolerant gardens. Jujubes also tolerate saline and alkaline soils, although they will produce more fruit and thrive in richer loam. They are resistant to insect pests and disease. Deciduous trees with a graceful, gnarled form, they generally grow from twelve to fifteen feet tall.

Sources differ as to the origins of the tree—some say Syria, others claim China. Regardless of their point of origin, jujubes are now grown in northern Africa, southern Europe, Russia, India, throughout the south and west of the United States and as far north as Pennsylvania and Oregon, as well as in the Middle East and China.

Jujube fruit ripens in late summer to early fall and resembles small apples. The skin is pale green that becomes mottled with red as the fruit matures. It has a crisp texture and sweet flavor. After ripening, the fruit may be left on the tree, where it will dry and become red dates. The dried fruit will last indefinitely—no preservative required.

According to traditional Chinese herbal medicine, red dates, or *hong zao,* clear the nose, throat and sinuses. In Britain, jujube was used as a remedy for sore throats and coughs. Lozenges that included the fruit were called jujubes (JOO-joo-bees), and the name came to refer to any lozenge or soft sweet. The correct pronunciation of the fruit is "joo-JOO-bee" according to Roger Meyer, who grows jujubes commercially in Valley Center, California.

There are 400 varieties of jujubes. 'Li' and 'Lang' are the two most commonly available cultivars. They were originally introduced to

California by Frank Meyer of Meyer lemon fame. He imported improved Chinese varieties to the Plant Introduction Station at Chico, California in the early 1900s.

'Li' has large, round fruit that grow up to three ounces in mid-August. The tree is many-branched, yet narrow and upright. The fruits are best eaten fresh. Sources recommend this as the best first jujube tree to have.

'Lang' has large, pear-shaped fruit that should be allowed to achieve full red color before eating. This fruit is one of the best to let dry on the tree.

'So,' a somewhat dwarfed tree, grows in a zig-zag branching pattern. At each stem node, new growth takes off at ninety degrees. Its shape is most striking in wintertime. It fruits mid-season.

'Topeka,' from eastern Kansas, has excellent, late season fruit.

Although eating and cooking with jujube has not caught on yet in the United States, in parts of the world jujube is an important fruit crop. In Jodhpur, India, the Central Arid Zone Research Institute has carried out a thirty-year research and development program and selected fifty cultivars for commercial development as a perennial fruit tree crop for arid lands. In India, 90,000 hectares of land (about 225,000 acres) and 300,000 people are engaged in jujube cultivation. For commercial cultivation, high productivity and the ability to be transported and stored are key factors. In China, the largest producer, dried jujube dates are used to flavor soups and salty dishes. In traditional Chinese medicine, uses extend well beyond that of a cold remedy.

In home gardens, a jujube tree can provide not only an attractive focal point, but also contribute to a habitat attractive to birds, that will compete with the gardener for the fruit. Edward Hagar sums up the attractions of jujubes, "Gardeners who visit my backyard garden-orchard in Thousand Oaks, California usually ask why I have so many jujube trees. My answer is easy: no other tree gives me so much pleasure for so little effort."

~

CHAPTER FIVE

~

Garden Maintenance

So What Is Organic Gardening?

~

BY DIANE LYNCH

The word organic simply means something that is or has been alive at one time, as opposed to inorganic, which has never been alive. Peat moss is organic because it is leaves and other plant matter that have been compressed in a peat bog, then harvested. Chemically speaking, organic matter contains carbon. Most rocks are largely inorganic because they are composed of minerals that were never alive, although some rocks contain fossils of organic nature. Because these terms are very broad there has been much confusion about what "organic" means when it's bandied about on all kinds of labels. The other day I bought some bagged steer manure and was taken in by the word "organics" as part of the company name. Well, this manure does not meet the official definition of organic because the cattle that produced it were not raised on organically-grown grain, which would have been proudly stated on the package, but technically it's certainly organic by the dictionary definition.

Organic gardening does not use synthetic chemicals and water-soluble fertilizers and pesticides, but relies on building healthy soil by adding organic matter and naturally derived, as opposed to manufactured, pesticides such as sulfur and copper. Be aware that some approved organic products are toxic to bees, caterpillars and fish.

From the thirties to the forties, use of synthetic fertilizers more than doubled and after World War II use almost doubled again, but their use dates back as far as the 1840s. The general "waste not/want not" philosophy of people prior to the late twentieth century meant that garden waste was recycled back into the garden either by composting or simply turning it back into the soil. In the days before widespread garbage collection, it made no sense to haul garden waste to the dump. Since many people kept chickens and other farm animals in suburban areas, these manures were recycled into the garden and the need for chemical fertilizers was small except in farming operations. After the war, chemical companies began marketing an array of garden products to keep insects and plant pests under control, as well as synthetic fertilizers, which were easier to use than manures. As the downsides of these products became evident and publicized in books such as Rachel Carson's *Silent Spring,* people began to realize that natural products might be better. People such as Helen and Scott Nearing wrote about simple, sustainable living in *Living the Good Life,* as they inspired others to become self-sufficient.

Farmer and publisher J. I. Rodale coined the term "organic" in the late forties and emphasized building soil fertility by working in organic matter and using cover crops. These techniques would build healthy soil to produce healthy plants, which were more nutritious and resistant to pests and disease. Before Rodale, Rudolph Steiner of Germany started a system of biodynamic farming which emphasized animals and composting as the key to a sustainable, balanced farm ecosystem. The earthy, independent, organic types who adhered to these philosophies were treated as a fringe group by many mainstream gardeners, university authorities and even Secretary of Agriculture Earl Butz in the 1970s.

By the 1980s, it became evident that it was time for an organic standard to be written to give consistency to the hype that was pitched on food products in particular. In 1990, both the federal government and the State of California passed organic standard acts. The California act was modeled after the standard established by California Certified Organic Farmers (CCOF) in 1973, one of the first organizations to certify organic farms in North America. Organic farmers must follow strict rules about soil supplements and chemical use and open their farms to periodic inspections.

Gardening Organically

So you want to garden organically? Start with eliminating synthetic fertilizers, which are petroleum products, don't amend the soil and can contaminate the soil as well as local water supplies with excessive salts. Instead, use organic supplements including:

- manures: available bagged, ready to use, or possibly free from stables or dairies. Fresh manure should be composted before use. Be careful not to overuse manure, which is high in salts that can be detrimental to plant growth.
- green manures or cover crops: usually legumes planted in the fall and then mowed or tilled into the soil as flowering begins.
- bloodmeal: available bagged at nurseries, a good source of nitrogen.
- bonemeal: high in phosphorus, slow release, reduces soil acidity.
- cottonseed meal: source of nitrogen, acidifies.
- fish meal and/or emulsion: source of nitrogen and phosphorus.
- phosphate rock: slow release phosphorus and micronutrients, use with manure.

Start a compost system, which can have three bins so you turn the compost into the next bin to speed the process, or use the low-tech method and simply let it sit until it decomposes into brown crumbly matter to put in the garden. Adding organic matter from compost or allowing leaves and other natural debris to decompose under plants will restore your soil to a natural ecosystem better able to take care of itself, with fewer pest problems.

Reduce your reliance on pesticides and herbicides. Soil and water contamination are common side effects of these chemicals and some leave persistent residues such as arsenic (treated wood), lead, mercury and copper—toxic to us as well as the animals that frequent our gardens. Instead, become an observant gardener and practice less toxic techniques to combat problems:

- Observe carefully and regularly what's going on when something isn't thriving. Go outside at night with a flashlight to look for and destroy slugs and snails. Use a hand lens to observe what's on the underside of problematic leaves.

* Learn to identify pests by taking bugs to the County Extension Service for identification if you can't figure out who's who. Most insects and bugs are beneficial and part of a healthy ecosystem.
* Adopt a tolerance for damage, realizing that complete control means you've wiped out many of the good guys also.
* Cultural practices such as removing diseased plant parts, proper watering, and not overfertilizing can reduce many problems.
* Non-disruptive materials will manage many insect pests: insecticidal oil, insecticidal soap and *Bacillus thuringiensis* (Bt) are useful and less toxic than conventional pesticides. Use only as specified on the label.

What's the Best Mulch for Your Garden?

~

BY JANE SCURICH

As the days grow longer and the sunshine beckons us outdoors, the gardener's "to do" list seems never ending. One item common to most all our lists is mulch. After the winter snow and rain have broken down the mulch we so carefully heaped on our gardens last fall, it's time for a mulch renewal. Most of us know the myriad benefits a layer of mulch offers, but, as a reminder, mulch helps to:

- suppress weed growth
- prevent compaction of the soil
- prevent erosion
- conserve soil moisture
- act as a nutrition source
- add a decorative element to the planting beds

With all the wonderful benefits offered by mulching, the question arises, "What is the best mulch?" Unfortunately, there is no one answer. There is no single, all-purpose mulch that works in all situations. Sometimes we choose a variety of mulches for different areas of our garden. What we like best for the vegetable patch may not be what we choose for the perennial beds. Gardeners have mulched for years using products from their own trees and lawns. Raking leaves in the fall and building a thick layer over the vegetable bed to protect the soil from heavy snow and rain and allowing the leaves to decompose is a long-standing practice for many. Those of us with smaller yards and planting areas may not have as much raw material to work with, so we purchase mulch in quantities appropriate to our needs.

Probably the most common mulch is bark chips. It is readily available, comes in various sizes, is affordable, and pleasant to the eye.

Most of these chips are dyed a neutral color such as redwood. On the downside, it is very attractive to snails and slugs as they enjoy the moisture it retains and the color serves as a nice camouflage for them. When you're shopping for bark mulch, be sure to pick up a container of an iron phosphate snail and slug deterrent such as Sluggo or Escar-Go and use as directed on your freshly mulched beds. Some types of mold and fungus may be encouraged to grow if the chips stay too damp. Use a rake to fluff it up and redistribute the bark every few months.

A related product is shredded cedar or "gorilla hair." As a gorilla's coat helps shed water and protect it from the elements, the bark with the similar name also tends to shed water, making it a good choice for a hillside, but not so good for moisture-loving flower beds.

One lovely and very aromatic mulch is cocoa bean hulls. They are reputed to be very beneficial to roses. Unfortunately, they can be lethal to dogs who are very attracted to their sweet fragrance. They should only be used in enclosed areas where no dog will be visiting. Their beauty also carries a stiffer price tag than the bark products. Coca hulls should be used for spring and summer mulching, as they tend to mold in the shorter, moister days of fall and winter.

Straw and hay have many admirers as they break down rapidly and readily attract earthworms to the area to fertilize and aerate the soil. They are inexpensive and often free after Halloween events or country western parties. The bad news is that hay bales often include a variety of random weed seeds ready to populate your garden.

So how about using newspapers that typically end up on the curb in recycling bags? This is a very easy and inexpensive organic mulching process. Place two to six full sheets of newspaper around the base of the desired plant, about two inches away from the trunk. On top of the newspaper add a one- to two-inch layer of bark chips, compost, or grass clippings. Repeat the process when the original layer decomposes. The newspaper ink is not toxic to your garden.

Pine needles are abundantly used in some parts of the country, as their natural acidity benefits the acid-loving families of azaleas and rhododendrons. Nutshells of any kind are frequently used and are often available for free in the area where they grow. Crushed almond shells offer a pleasing blond color and their slightly sharp edges deter snails and slugs. Avoid using salted nutshells unless you boil them first to rid them of their salt content.

In addition to organic mulches, which offer the additional benefits of providing a nutrient source as they slowly break down, many people rely on inorganic products for mulching. Black plastic, recycled shredded rubber truck tires and gravel offer longer lasting alternatives and each has its own set of benefits and drawbacks

If you really want to have fun with your mulch and make an artistic statement as well, check out colored glass pebbles or the wide variety of colored bark available online. Dress your flowerbeds in your favorite team colors for baseball season!

Whether you choose your mulch based on weed control, economy, or visual enhancement, you are sure to reap benefits from your efforts.

Worm Composting in Small Spaces

~

BY LEE OLIPHANT

So you've tried composting. You bought or built a compost bin the size of a Volkswagen and placed it in the corner of your garden. You saved your lawn cuttings. You mixed in kitchen scraps, added dry leaf materials, and turned the pile diligently every few days to aerate the contents. In return for your efforts you got a bucketful of nice compost material to enrich your soil, provide a layer of mulch and give your plants a hardy meal.

While this endeavor is noble, you may want to try composting on a smaller, more concentrated, scale. Worm composting (or vermicomposting) gives you a real "bang for your buck," takes up little space, is easy, fun (you get attached to the little critters), and will provide you with rich worm castings that your plants and soil will love.

Worm composting is a low-maintenance method of recycling your kitchen scraps by providing a bin for "red wigglers" (*Eisenia foetida*). Not to be confused with the earthworms you find when digging in your garden (who, by the way, do not flourish in bins), these are a particular kind of worm with a voracious appetite that reproduce rapidly and have a propensity to thrive in confined quarters. These little worms can eat their weight in garbage every day. In return for your vegetable and fruit scraps, worms give you potent and valuable "black gold," or worm castings, the ultimate plant food for indoor and outdoor plants. This method of recycling your kitchen scraps is the perfect solution for people with small yards, apartment dwellers, or for classrooms.

You will need only a few things to begin worm composting: a simple worm bin, newspaper bedding, kitchen scraps, and worms. You will need a space for the bin that is protected, since worms thrive in

132

temperatures between 50° and 75°F. Some options for bin locations are in the garage, basement, on a shady patio, under a deck, or in a garden shed.

THE WORM BIN

While there are commercially-made bins available, you might want to begin your worm composting with a five- to ten-gallon plastic tub with a lid that snaps shut to keep out foraging critters that also love garbage. Worms like the dark so an opaque bin is best.

For ventilation, drill small holes in the sides of the bin no more than four inches down from the top. You can space or stagger the holes two to four inches apart. Some worm composters drill a few holes in the bottom of the bins to drain liquid if the worm bin becomes too moist. I prefer not to do this as you will have to keep the bin on a tray to catch the runoff. If your composting becomes too moist, just add dry strips of newspaper to the bottom layer of your compost to absorb the excess liquid.

BEDDING FOR YOUR WORMS

The natural habitat for red worms is in piles of fallen leaves above the soil surface. The best bedding for them is moist newspaper and cardboard, shredded. Any rough paper will do as long as it does not have colored ink. After you have wet the paper and it is well drained or wrung out (like a wrung-out sponge), separate the strips. Place it into the bin about one-third the way up the sides. Because worms don't have teeth, they need grit to help them digest. Add a handful of well-crushed eggshells, fine sand, or sawdust.

FOOD

A pound of red worms needs about a pound of scraps each week. Red worms will eat any part of fruit and vegetables. They like coffee grounds and filters, tea bags, and watermelon rind. Layer about a half-pound of scraps over the bedding. Do not put meat, oils, cat or dog feces, or dairy products in your worm bin. Worms should be fed about once a week but can go longer without food.

THE WORMS

"Red wigglers" can be purchased at garden centers, at bait shops or from suppliers on the internet. You will need less than one-half pound to begin your bin.

HARVESTING THE CASTINGS

Your worms should be separated from their castings about twice a year. There are two methods to do this. One is to push the decomposed material to one side of the bin and remake their bed with moist bedding and kitchen scraps on the other. Worms will migrate to the freshly filled side of the bin and you can scoop out the finished compost.

I prefer a second method, as my worms usually refuse to leave their present surroundings no matter how "green" it is on the other side of the bin. Place the bin under a bright light or in the sun. The worms will dive for darker quarters. After a few minutes remove the top inch of compost (sans worms) and repeat. If you find worm eggs (tiny strands of beads), pick them out and add to the new bedding. Repeat this process until the worms have migrated to the bottom of the bin and you have the compost you need. Refill the bin with fresh layers of moist bedding material and food.

Worm compost is very concentrated. Sprinkle and dig it into freshly cultivated soil. For potting mixes, mix one part worm compost to four parts potting mix. To fertilize plants, sprinkle worm compost around the base of plants before watering. You can also make a compost "tea" by putting it in a cloth bag and soaking it in water for a few days, then using the water on your plants.

There are many informational resources for worm composting. An excellent book on the subject is *Worms Eat My Garbage* by Mary Appelhoff. She also has a website: www.wormwoman.com. Another good resource for composting at home is MagicWorms.com.

Sheet Composting

~

BY CHARLOTTE TORGOVITSKY

In winter, most of my raised vegetable beds are given over to greens: dinosaur kale, perpetual spinach, arugula, lettuce and parsley, all grown to supplement family meals. One bed, though, of fava beans, is grown to supplement the soil. The seeds were planted in November, just as I picked the very last tomato, and quickly pushed up fat, juicy sprouts.

Like all legumes, fava beans fix nitrogen from the air onto nodules in their root systems, thereby adding to the fertility of the soil. The plants are now about a foot high, and I will cut them down and gently till them into the earth as "green manure," covering it all with a bed of straw. This is one method of sheet composting, and by early May, which is the optimum time to plant tomatoes where I live, decomposition will have occurred. The soil will be greatly enriched, and able to produce an abundant crop of the tomatoes, basil, and lemon cucumbers that the whole family loves in summer salads and gazpacho.

Sheet composting, in its various methods, is passive composting. There is a minimum amount of labor required, and results take time; but, in nature, compost happens!

In another method of sheet composting, materials trimmed from an established border are simply left there to decompose. This method is gratifying in a most practical sense. Why move materials to a composting site, just to move them back again, as a topdressing of finished compost?

The dry, dead stalks of perennials, such as asters, sedums and yarrows, that die back to the ground in winter, are simply cut and left around the base of various plants. Perennial grasses, which also need to be cut back once a year, are wonderful as sheet-composting materials, and can double as mulch. Cutting materials into smaller pieces will speed up the process somewhat, and give the layer a more uniform, mulch-like look. Sheet composted materials will take a year or more to break down, but a healthy and vigorously growing mixed border of perennials, grasses, and shrubs will soon grow to camouflage the compost materials.

Sheet composting can also be used to create new and fertile gardening sites. Land previously given over to ground covers such as ivy or vinca, or perhaps just assorted weeds, can be reclaimed, with time, by layering materials that will decompose in place.

Plants growing on the site will first need to be cut to the ground. Then cover the area with layers of corrugated cardboard and newspaper, and on top of this put a layer of manure. Leaves, grass clippings, and all sorts of plant materials can then be layered on top of the manure. Remember that the microorganisms doing the work need both carbon- and nitrogen-type materials, so try to build the layers using both browns (carbon-rich materials like dead leaves) and greens (nitrogen-rich materials such as grass clippings). For best results, do not use wood chips or other materials that take a long time to break down.

This is a good time to supplement the soil with various organic materials. Blood meal, soybean meal, or alfalfa pellets can be sprinkled in between the layers. Sheet composting also creates a good opportunity to add rock powders, which provide a range of micronutrients and minerals to the soil. These fertilizers are relatively insoluble, but the decaying process will help facilitate the release of their nutrients.

The area can be built up to a depth of a foot or more, and covered over with a layer of straw for a more uniform look. Decomposition takes time, so plan to sheet compost an area in fall; and don't think about planting it until the next spring, or early summer. By that time, the organic materials will have smothered the roots of plants previously growing on the site, and decomposed sufficiently to be worked into the soil.

You will now have soil rich in organic materials, and all the micro-organisms that help support healthy plant growth. Sheet composting is also a great way to deal with heavy clay soil.

Everyone who gardens can compost, and your plants and our environment will benefit from it. Organic materials are returned to the earth, building a rich and fertile topsoil that retains moisture and oxygen. Such healthy soil is the underlying support of the entire web of life, and a resource center for healthy plants.

Weed Identification and Control

~

by Barbara J. Euser

The plentiful rains this spring have produced an especially vibrant crop of weeds in my garden. In between showers, I have been pulling them out. As I work, I contemplate what I know about the various species. Knowing the enemy in this case is essential to controlling it.

Weeds can be defined as any misplaced plants. For example, a tomato plant is welcome in the kitchen vegetable garden, but is a weed in the front flower border. However, weeds are also defined by their characteristic competitiveness, persistence and perniciousness. Weeds produce abundant seeds that may survive in a dormant state for long periods of time. They establish populations rapidly, easily occupy disturbed sites and have developed multiple methods for spreading vegetatively. They are tough enough to out-compete the plants we are trying to cultivate in our gardens. Thus, we engage in the ongoing struggle to bring them under control.

Weed Identification

Identifying weeds is key to controlling them. It is important to understand their life cycles, how they grow and develop. Just as other plants in our gardens, weeds can be divided into annuals, biennials and perennials. Annuals grow, set seed and die in one year or less. They may be either winter annuals that germinate in the fall, live through the winter and produce seed in the winter and spring, or summer annuals that germinate in the spring and produce seed in summer or fall. Winter annuals include mallow, groundsel and annual bluegrass. Summer annuals include lambs quarters, spotted spurge, crabgrass and pigweed.

Biennials take two years to complete their life cycles. In the first year, they produce leaves, stems and roots. In the spring and summer of the second year, they flower, set seed and die. They are easier to control than annuals because we usually discover and eliminate them from our gardens during their first year of growth, before they have a chance to set seed and spread. Examples of biennial weeds include mullein, bull thistle, oxtongue and shepherd's purse.

Perennial weeds live longer than two years and develop more extensive root systems than annuals or biennials. Young perennials may be pulled or hoed out. However, once they are established, they are difficult to eradicate. Simple perennials, such as dandelions, reproduce only by seed. Creeping perennials, such as wood sorrel (*Oxalis*) and Bermuda grass, spread aggressively via underground structures including stolons, rhizomes, tubers and bulbs. They may be dormant over the winter and send out new shoots in the spring. Other perennial weeds are nutsedge, broom, bindweed and poison oak.

From the point of view of plant taxonomy, weeds can be divided into broadleafs (dicots) or grasses (monocots). Thus, there are annual, biennial and perennial broadleafs and annual, biennial and perennial grasses.

As I work to eliminate the weeds in my garden, I try to pull out annuals before they have a chance to go to seed. Biennials must go at first appearance. I dig out perennials like dandelions and *Oxalis* and poison oak, capturing as much of the root systems as possible. Knowing something about weeds' life cycles increases my understanding of their characteristics. It doesn't make the work easier, but by putting names to the weeds and learning something about them, I develop a relationship with them. As I learn more about all the plants in my garden, I find more pleasure in the endless endeavor of creating and maintaining it.

WEED CONTROL

As interesting as it is to know the names of various weeds and whether they are annuals, biennials or perennials, my real motivation in getting to know them is to determine how to control them. I would like to eliminate weeds completely from my garden, but given the competitive advantages weeds enjoy, producing thousand of seeds or hundreds of underground tubers each year (one yellow nutsedge plant can make 400 new tubers in one year), I will settle for some level of weeds I can control using the various means available.

There are four basic categories of weed control: cultural, mechanical, physical and chemical.

Cultural

The point of cultural weed control is to modify the garden environment to increase the desirable plants' competitive edge while decreasing the competitive advantage of weeds. The selection of plants is critical. By choosing among the many plants that naturally thrive in our garden's climate, we immediately improve the garden's edge over weeds.

The condition of the garden's soil is another cultural factor. Know whether your garden soil is clay or sand or loam and choose plants that prefer your existing soil type, or modify the soil by adding organic matter such as compost to make it a better home for the plants you prefer.

Prepare the soil for planting by loosening it so oxygen will be available for plants' roots to grow. Similarly, reduce soil compaction by watching where you step in the garden. Trampling the garden squeezes the spaces out of the soil, spaces necessary for the flow of air and water, and growth of roots.

Proper irrigation is another cultural factor in weed control. Overwatering may encourage the germination of weed seeds, whereas underwatering may stress plants and allow weeds to move in.

Lawns should be watered deeply and infrequently to discourage weeds such as crabgrass. Thatch should be removed if it gets over one-half-inch thick. Mowing height is also important. A key rule is to never remove more than one-third of the leaf blade in a simple mowing. "Scalping" a lawn allows weeds to germinate and grow.

MECHANICAL

These are the tried-and-true, time-honored techniques of weed control: hoeing, cultivating, hand pulling, mowing and chopping. They are non-polluting and require no elaborate equipment. In my garden, combined with the cultural and physical weed control methods I also employ, some time each week spent hand pulling and digging keeps weeds down to a tolerable level.

For annual weeds, the main objective is to get them out before they set seed. Using a dandelion digger, I cut them below their crowns, just beneath the soil level. Perennial weeds require repeated digging out. The theory is that eventually their roots will be starved for food and will die out. Persistence is the key. It may require several years of digging up perennial weeds to starve them out.

An old rhyme, "Water, wait, then cultivate," describes a mechanical system for controlling weeds. Before planting a bed, prepare it to finished grade, then water it to germinate the weed seeds that are already present. Wait until the weeds sprout, then, using a hoe, get rid of them. For best results, repeat the process a second time. When you do plant your garden seeds, disturb the soil as little as possible to avoid bringing more weed seeds to the surface.

PHYSICAL

Physical weed control means placing a barrier between weed seeds and the sun. Without light, there is no photosynthesis and weeds can't grow. A physical barrier is usually mulch. Mulch may be organic, such as ground bark, straw or compost, or inorganic, such as commercial weed blocks or black polyethylene plastic.

Mulch is a very effective way to control weeds. I have been using shredded bark in my garden for several years. Over time it breaks down, adding organic matter to the soil, and I add a new layer. I can tell how effective it is because in the farthest corner of my garden, where the mulch is very thin, a significant number of weeds flourish. I have pulled them out again this year, but putting down a thick, three- to six-inch layer of mulch would save me a lot of time next spring.

Mulch also saves water. With a covering of mulch, soil stays moist longer, so adjust watering accordingly. Overwatering may result in root rot development from Phytophthora or Pythium fungi.

CHEMICAL

Chemical weed control, that is use of herbicides, should be the last resort. Herbicides are organic and inorganic chemicals that kill plants. They may be sprayed on weed foliage or applied to the soil. They may be pre-emergent, or soil-residual herbicides, that prevent the germination of weed seeds, or post-emergent, applied to weed foliage. Post-emergent herbicides may be contact herbicides that kill only the parts of plants they touch, or systemic herbicides that are absorbed into the plant and move through the plant's conductive tissues to affect another site, such as the plant's roots.

Herbicides may be nonselective, killing all vegetation, or selective, killing only susceptible species (presumably the weeds) and not damaging the tolerant species (the garden plants). Unfortunately, selectivity is relative, not absolute, and environmental conditions may make tolerant species susceptible to even selective herbicides. And herbicides we use in our gardens may end up polluting our water.

We may never completely eliminate weeds in our gardens, but by understanding something about weeds and the various means available to control them—cultural, mechanical, physical and chemical—we may transform them into less formidable foes.

Keep Pests at Bay, Don't Poison Earth

~

BY JULIE WARD CARTER

Are you tired of ants enjoying your home and garden more than you do? Are you tired of spiders lurking in every crevice and corner of your home and garden? Are you tired of spraying and re-spraying just to have these unwelcome guests return? Spraying is quick, easy, and cheap and makes you feel like you've solved the pest problem. But you haven't because chemical treatments are temporal in solving pest problems. In most cases, making environmental changes and implementing Integrated Pest Management principles in the household, garden or public lands can significantly reduce the need to apply chemicals.

So what is an Integrated Pest Management (IPM) program? IPM is a way of thinking about an innovative approach to pest management decision-making that integrates understanding of the pest's or disease's life cycle, its biology and human-pest interaction. IPM uses a combination of a wide range of pest management strategies to avoid pest problems—of which pesticides are usually the last choice.

IPM programs are being implemented throughout the United States. Marin County, just north of San Francisco, provides an illustrative example of how different agencies can coordinate efforts to reduce the use of toxic chemicals.

The Marin County Stormwater Pollution Prevention Program (MCSTOPPP) is concerned with the overuse of pesticides because these chemicals end up in local creeks, bays and wastewater treatment plants. Created in 1993 with a major focus on "preventing stormwater pollution and protecting water quality in creeks and wetlands," according to Gina Purin, MCSTOPPP's Community Outreach and Education Coordinator, this organization successfully cooperates with the University of California Cooperative Extension Master Gardeners in reducing or completely avoiding pesticide use in homes and gardens. MCSTOPP is also working with local nurseries to help customers identify less-toxic alternatives by adding "shelf-talkers" next to such products.

In 1998, the Marin County Board of Supervisors approved Ordinance #3286 with its goal of a 75 percent reduction of pesticide use in public spaces. An appointed IPM Commission is actively working to achieve this reduction. "We have made big improvements on reduction in pesticide use," says Dave Hattem of the Marin County Park Division. "We have reduced pesticide use by 83 percent in public spaces managed by the county staff."

Since 1995, Stacy Carlsen, Marin County Agricultural Commissioner, has developed an aggressive program that implements IPM principles in classrooms and on school grounds. His office established a "Pest Management Alliance Project" that made "Marin County schools a model program for legislation on the Healthy School Act," according to Commissioner Carlsen.

We buy pesticides offered over-the-counter in retail stores either preformed for immediate use or in small bottles or containers requiring dilution to kill pests, diseases or weeds. A single use seems harmless, but if these "tiny bits" of chemicals are washed away with rain from thousands of houses to the local creeks and bays, they become a serious threat to our water supply. This concerns the Coalition for a Pesticide Free Marin (comprised of city, county, state and school organizations and Marin residents) that promotes pest management according to IPM principles or gardening completely without pesticides.

About 99 percent of insects in the garden are beneficial, including those "obnoxious" ants and spiders. Repeated applications of insecticides kill not only pests but also beneficial insects. As beneficial insects disappear from the garden, pests return faster and re-infest rose, tomato, or other plants and the vicious cycle of these chemicals' overuse continues. "The Marin County Parks Department reduced pesticide use by 83 percent on county land. We should also achieve this level in our cities, schools and residences and live in a healthier environment," stated Judi Shils from the Coalition for a Pesticide Free Marin. Additionally, pests and diseases become resistant—today it takes from two to five applications of pesticides to reduce a pest's population to a tolerable level, whereas in the 1970s just one application accomplished the same effect according to well-documented statistics. Gina Purin says, "Consider Diazinon, a common household pesticide that has been available over-the-counter for about forty years and has now been removed from most store shelves. Just one grain of seed coated with Diazinon is enough to kill a small bird, such as a finch, that relies mainly on seeds for food."

There is a whole array of preventive methods for treating pests or diseases that are successful and do not use chemicals, including composting, irrigating, aerating the soil, fertilizing, mulching, planting insect-attracting plants, and planting proper plant species (variety) at the right time and in the right place. If you want to help keep local waters cleaner, protect your family from unnecessary exposure to toxic chemicals and create a long-lasting stability in your garden, anywhere in the United States you may contact your local County Extension Agent. Ask about IPM pest management strategy workshops that cover sanitation, habitat modification, biological, mechanical and safe chemical controls and emphasize prevention rather than therapeutic strategies. Using the principles of IPM, we can create a cleaner and safer environment.

Uninvited Guests

~

BY JANE SCURICH

As the daylight hours dwindle and our hopes for a warm Indian summer bring plans for one last perfect picnic, the ever-present party crasher reaches peak population levels. The tiny Argentine ant doesn't wait for an invitation. He somehow knows when food and beverages will appear to fulfill his insatiable hunger. In hot weather, this one-eighth-inch crawling critter builds nests under trees and in other shady locations (think the perfect picnic spot). In the fall, he relocates his colony to sunnier spots. Populations swell in midsummer and early fall. So chances are, if you're enjoying yourself outside, you have some crawling companions.

Reportedly, the first scout of *Iridomyrmex humilis* arrived on a coffee ship from Argentina that docked in New Orleans in 1891. Following the old adage, "Go West Young Man!" he started a long journey which has left his progeny across the United States and which found its way to your and my backyard.

Learning to appreciate the benefits offered by this hardy species is far better than grabbing a can of toxic substance and spraying indiscriminately. Ants are important natural enemies of many insect pests. They provide an ecological cleansing service, recycle dead animal and vegetable material and aerate the soil. With these credentials, we need to focus on living with them in a mutually acceptable format. Personally, I do my best to avoid the use of pesticides of any type. I am constantly on the lookout for pest damage in my garden and I try to correct problems using natural controls. To that end, I have adopted the following environmentally acceptable behavior criteria for ants:

- You will not come in my house. To discourage you, I will be diligent about caulking around my doors and windows. I will keep my pet's food stored and her serving container clean.
- I will use good sanitation protocol, storing food in sealed containers, and cleaning up sticky spills.
- If you are a scout (the explorer sent to find food and report back), you will be history. It is my job to eliminate you and clean your entry path with soap so as to remove your chemical trail. Sorry.
- If you build your nest in my potted plants, I will put the entire pot into a large container of water and I will provide you with a footbridge so that your queen, your workers, and your family can relocate—preferably, away from my patio.
- Choosing to farm scale on my Kefir lime was a major no-no. Tanglefoot is on my shelves if you try that again.
- I will leave you to do your good work: recycle, aerate, be all that you can be. I will employ all manner of IPM (Integrated Pest Management) strategies to allow us to coexist. But, if you come into my greenhouse this winter, you may force me into the first line of chemical defense: the boric acid ant stake, and I will use it if necessary. You have been warned.

Now that my local ant population and I have reached an understanding of sorts, I will elaborate a bit on my personal plans for ant control. "Farming" refers to the practice in which ants protect scale, aphid and mealybugs from natural predators in order to feast on the honeydew they excrete. Tanglefoot is a sticky material that may be applied to the base of trees to discourage the trafficking of ants. Follow the directions carefully and be sure to apply the product in the early morning or late evening. Do not leave an ant colony stranded on the upper limbs of your tree at midday. They will establish a new colony! If you come to the end of your rope, if you cannot tolerate one more ant: stop. Do not spray. Try a bait with either boric acid or arsenic. Use the bait with caution, out of reach from children and pets, and remove the bait when the infestation is over.

My personal hope is that you will learn to live with the Argentine ant. He was here before us, he will undoubtedly outlive us, and, all things considered, is he really that big a problem?

Foiling Deer Gracefully

~

BY BARBARA J. EUSER

Gentle, graceful deer emerge from the edge of the forest to graze in our hillside meadow. I harbor this image from years when I lived in Golden Gate Canyon in the foothills above Denver, Colorado. Here in Marin, deer emerge from the greenbelt to graze in my garden, which I do not appreciate at all. It took several years, during which the deer devoured dozens of newly planted flowers and shrubs, before I began to understand the art of deer-resistant landscaping. I still make mistakes, but there are a number of plants that deer are not interested in eating. I have incorporated these in the deer-accessible section of the garden. The deer still roam through freely, but they inflict less damage.

When trying to determine whether or not a plant might be deer resistant, it helps to think like a hungry deer. Sharp, stickery plants scratch the throat. Long needles can get caught on the way down. Blade-like leaves are equally hard to swallow. Strong-smelling foliage, even though it might be the right texture, is off-putting. Plants that grow too close to the ground are hard to pull out, and if they have much of an odor, aren't worth the effort.

Plants that deer don't like to eat come in a variety of colors and shapes and range from trees to ground covers. Based on the categories of unappetizing plants described above, here are the plants in my garden that deer do not eat.

Sharp, stickery plants include asparagus fern and juniper. As anyone who has handled aparagus fern knows, those light, feathery fronds conceal sharp spines. Juniper is an obvious throat-scratcher and I have a low-growing one spreading as a ground cover and another developing into a handsome specimen bush. Others in this category not in my own garden, but that I have observed growing unmolested nearby, are handsome magenta-leaved barberry and sprawling cotoneaster.

The long needles of my grevillea deter the deer. At this time of year, it is covered with intricate pink and cream blossoms and appears especially graceful and delicate. My rosemary is filled with tiny blue flowers and will continue to bloom for months. The fragrant needles, so highly prized in cooking, hold no attraction for the deer.

Scattered throughout the garden are clumps of fortnight lilies, also called African iris. I prize them for their sword-like leaves, their upright form and their delicate blooms. They bloom once every two weeks, hence their name. The clumps may be divided easily and the new, smaller sections grow vigorously. Although their leaves are not as rigid as African iris, the bearded iris in my garden have likewise not been eaten by the deer.

Strong-smelling foliage is also of no interest to local deer. My Spanish lavender grows unmolested. I have read that some varieties of lavender are not deer resistant and the other varieties of lavender I grow are in a deer-protected part of the garden. However, I can vouch for Spanish lavender. Its deep purple blooms are short-lived, but its gray-green foliage is attractive year round. Santolina is another gray-leaved, deer-resistant plant. Soon it will be covered by tiny yellow blossoms that are lovely while they last. They are also an aggravation to deadhead, but the plant looks much better when I take the time to do it. Mint is an example of a fragrant plant deer do not eat. I let it run rampant in one corner of the garden and although I see deer prints in the soil, they leave the mint alone.

Three ground covers thrive despite the deer. Wooly thyme is fragrant and that may be the deterrent. Woodland strawberries are attractive to me, happily not at all to the deer. Similarly, *Vinca minor*, with its pale blue star flowers, is of no interest for grazing purposes. Another apparently delicate flower that deer do not eat is the vibrant orange California poppy. Paired with Spanish lavender, for a few weeks in spring it is stunning.

My calla lily, which has provided me with cut flowers for our entryway table for two months now, is completely unappealing to the deer. The plant will die back during the summer and the leaves will become limp and brown and mushy. At that point, I also find it unappealing. But the flowers bring me so much pleasure during their season, I plan to divide it when it goes dormant this year and plant a few more clumps.

Shrubs the deer don't eat include heavenly bamboo (*Nandina*), oleander, Pride of Madeira (*Echium*), yew and rhododendron. Partially concealed by my white rhododendron is a large white azalea. The deer do not eat it, perhaps because it is a large shrub. I mistakenly thought this meant that azaleas in general were unattractive to deer. That is not the case in my garden. The new azaleas I planted were chewed voraciously by the deer, some to death. Belatedly I covered them with deer netting. Several are now blooming pink, red and orange. But I don't like the looks of netting and when I remove it, they will once again be vulnerable.

Trees that deer avoid in my garden are oak, pine, toyon, and *Podocarpus*.

Planting a garden attractive to ourselves and unattractive to deer requires thought and careful selection, but it can be done, gracefully.

Amazing Survivors: Rats and Mice

~

BY DIANE LYNCH

Rats and mice have been a problem for humans as long as we've been around. Because they are well adapted to our behavior and needs, they are incredible survivors and are all but impossible to eliminate. They thrive in crowded, unsanitary conditions as well as clean places—urban, suburban and rural situations alike. Since they will eat almost anything we eat, they are well fed in our home gardens and compost piles.

A female rat has a life span of about a year in the wild and during that time can fledge eighty-four young. Rats can tunnel four feet into the ground, swim a half-mile, walk across telephone wires, flatten themselves and slip under a door or through a crack, survive a fall of fifty feet. With these abilities, we are lucky just to keep them under control.

Rats and mice are more than socially unacceptable. They get into our food sources and contaminate them with urine and feces. They will gnaw plastic, paper, books, wood, clothing, even wiring, all of which are used as nesting matter. They can carry harmful parasites like fleas, mites and worms as well as spread many diseases, such as salmonellosis (bacterial food poisoning), leptospirosis (spread through rat urine), Lyme disease, even bubonic plague. Deer and house mice are known vectors of Hanta virus.

We cannot afford to be too casual about cleaning up after rodents and even our pets. Anytime you have to be in contact with any animal waste, including rodent infestations and dog, cat or bird waste, you should wear gloves and mask, spray the area with an antibacterial spray, wait fifteen minutes and then use a damp cloth or paper towels to clean up. Never sweep or vacuum, as this will spread potentially toxic dust.

Two of the types of rats that commonly infest gardens are:

* Roof rat (*Rattus rattus*) is mostly black with some gray, thirteen to eighteen inches total length, with the tail longer than the head and body combined. It's a good climber as the name implies and typically nests in attics, walls, vines, or trees.
* Norway rat (*Rattus norvegicus*) is mostly brown and about the same length as the roof rat, but heavier, with the tail shorter than the head and body. It's more common, has wider distribution, and nests under buildings, in woodpiles, dumps, yard junk, shrubs and ground cover.

There are several species of garden mice including:

* House mouse (*Mus musculus*) which is sandy brown when it lives outdoors and dark gray indoors, and is similar in appearance to the roof rat but five to eight inches in length. Not considered as serious a problem as rats, these mice do nevertheless contaminate food and gnaw on wiring and other inappropriate items.
* Deer mouse (*Peromyscus maniculatus*), similar in size to the house mouse, has a brown upper body and white undersides, with a bicolored tail.
* Meadow mouse or vole (*Microtus californicus*) is distinguished by its short tail. Typically inhabiting wildlands, they do not usually enter homes, but can be a problem in the garden as they dine on vegetables, fruit tree bark and landscape plants. Their gnawing can kill young trees.

Fall and winter are prime mouse and rat migration times as they move indoors to escape cold and rain. Because they are nocturnal, they can become well established and difficult to eradicate. Mice in particular forage only short distances, typically ten to twenty-five feet, from their nest and it is important to use control measures as close to nests as possible. Because they prefer being near walls or hedges, traps or baits should be placed in these areas. Since they are curious and will investigate new objects in their sphere, control devices which are not at first successful can be moved to improve the catch rate.

Mice feed on a wide variety of foods but prefer seeds and cereal grains as well as foods high in fat and protein such as nuts, bacon, butter and sweets. They are "nibblers" and may make twenty to thirty visits to different food sites each night. Rats, in contrast, are creatures of habit and very suspicious of change.

Thwarting Rodents' Requirements

Control of rats and mice is an ongoing process of thwarting some or all of their needs: food, water, shelter. Our gardens are a buffet if we plant for wildlife such as birds. Plants that produce berries or seeds are ideal rodent food. Clean up around the garden, thin ivy, vines and shrubs and store lawn seed and bone meal in secure containers. Mouse and rat populations typically run in four-year cycles in response to seasonal food availability, but because we have year-round food outside, these cycles have ceased to be relevant.

Birdfeeders and pet bowls are a direct cause of the population explosion in rodents. Birdfeeders are built-in bait stations as seed drops to the ground. Feed birds on a patio where you can sweep up debris frequently. Empty and clean pet bowls after feeding and clean up pet droppings, as excrement can provide food for rodents. Cover garbage securely and manage compost piles to speed decomposition or elevate a foot or more off the ground. Obvious sources of water, such as leaky faucets or pet water bowls outside, can be repaired or eliminated.

Because mice can slip through a hole the size of a dime, our houses can be easy to penetrate. Check your foundation, vents in roof, eaves and foundation and utility pipes for holes and cracks that need patching. Use hardware cloth or sheet metal for patching large areas; small cracks can be stuffed with steel wool and filled with expanding foam. Ivy is one of the best homes for rats and mice, enabling them to forage while they remain concealed, so keep it thinned. Untrimmed palm trees also provide apartment house potential.

TRAPS AND TOXIC BAIT

The main control methods are various traps and toxic baits. Traps, such as the old-fashioned snap traps baited with favorite foods, like peanut butter and gumdrops, are effective in controlling rodents. One of the best, easiest to use, and sanitary is the Rat Zapper, a plastic box with batteries which instantly electrocutes rats or mice. These things really work and you can simply carry the box out to a visible location and deposit the critter for the hawks or vultures to eat. Encouraging raptors is another topic, but there is a lot of information about building barn owl (who eat an average of one gopher or rat per night) nesting boxes available on websites and through organizations such as the Audubon Society. There are also multiple catch traps (Ketch-All), which hold up to a dozen critters, available at hardware stores. Glue traps seem needlessly cruel. If you have rats, traps can be "pre-baited" without being set so they get used to them; you can then set them for real a few days later.

Rodenticides are typically anticoagulants in bait pouches. The problem with baits is that the rodents can die in inaccessible places, creating smelly problems. Dogs in particular find rodent bait tasty so the baits must be kept out of reach of pets, wildlife, and children. Follow directions to the letter.

If you have rats or mice, your neighbors do also, so have a neighborhood meeting and share information about how to control them. Severe infestations may require the services of a pest control company.

Pruning Shrubs and Vines

~

BY WILLIAM BENTLEY

Shrubs and vines are an essential part of any garden. They complement the trees, perennials, and annuals and, in many cases, serve as the anchor in the garden structure. We want them to be healthy and look their best. Many plants require little or no pruning; others must be pruned each year. Pruning is important to direct plant growth, provide light, increase flower production, control size, increase vigor, repair damage and remove disease.

How Do Plants Grow?

The natural growth pattern of the shrub or vine determines its shape and size. Most plant growth occurs in the terminal buds at the end of the branch. As the plant grows, it also forms lateral buds where a leaf is attached (nodes). Each node will have one to three buds, depending on the plant's leafing pattern. A hormone controls the growth of the lateral buds. This is called apical dominance. When a terminal bud is removed, it disrupts the apical dominance and creates growth in the lateral buds below the cut. The lateral bud immediately below the cut will then become the terminal bud. The leafing patterns of plants are alternate (one bud), opposite (two buds) or whorled (three or more buds).

Where to Cut?

For alternate leafing patterns, a pruning cut should be one-quarter inch above the bud you want to retain. If a large space is left between the terminal bud and the cut, this will encourage disease. The cut should slope away from the terminal bud to allow rain runoff. For opposite and whorled leafing patterns, make a flat cut one-quarter inch above the terminal buds. By selecting the buds you want to retain, you control the growth and direction of the plant. Cut carefully to accomplish your desired result.

How Much to Cut?

Pruning disrupts apical dominance and directs growth into the buds that are retained. It also stimulates growth. Pruning cuts are either heading or thinning. Heading cuts are used to reduce the size of the plant, create side growth, control direction, produce vigor and increase flower production. Heading cuts include shearing, pinching, and deadheading, since the result disrupts the apical dominance of the plant. Thinning cuts are used to remove diseased wood and cross branching, repair damage, increase vigor and flower production, provide additional light and air movement as well as to create side growth. Each plant has its own characteristics. For example, butterfly bush (*Buddleia*), tree mallow (*Lavatera*), and hydrangea can be cut back severely each year and will grow back to the same size and produce flowers. Other plants do well if thinned each year by removing a certain amount of branches, for example, heavenly bamboo (*Nandina*) and oleander.

When pruning, follow guidelines for the specific shrub or tree. And keep in mind that most of us tend to prune too lightly. Plants have survived for years after being pruned by those notorious headers, deer. Shrubs and vines have an estimated life just like humans. If you plan to renovate an old shrub or vine through heavy pruning, it would be wise to do this over two to three years. Otherwise, your efforts to invigorate an old plant may not produce the desired result.

When to Prune?

The time to prune depends on the characteristics of the plant and your objectives. Many shrubs and vines are pruned according to when they bloom. Generally, spring flowering plants flower on old wood and are best pruned during the dormant season or after they bloom. Examples of spring flowering shrubs and vines are *Viburnum*, bush anemone (*Carpenteria*), *Abelia*, *Pieris*, mock orange (*Philadelphus*), trumpet vine (*Campsis*), jasmine, honeysuckle (*Lonicera*), and non-repeat-flowering roses.

Summer and autumn flowering plants usually bloom on new wood and are pruned in late winter or early spring after the risk of frost, but before bud break. Examples of summer or autumn flowering plants are butterfly bush, bougainvillea, tree mallow, repeat flowering roses, fuchsias, lantana, heavenly bamboo, potato vine (*Solanum*), Russian sage (*Perovskia*) and salvias.

CHAPTER SIX

Cycle of Seasons

Putting the Garden to Bed

~

by Maryrose Whelan

Before winter arrives, it's time to clean the garden. It needn't be hard—it's all a question of where to begin.

Did our recent storms give you a bonus of pine needles? They make lovely mulch for the rhododendrons and azaleas. Or for any other acid-loving plants for that matter. So rake up the fallen rhododendron leaves and replace with pine needles.

Check the perennials. Remove the top third of the agastache and the gauras and shear the lavenders if you have not already done so. Cut back the dianthus and Shasta daisies. If you have autumn blooming clematis, it has bloomed and faded. Cut it down. Off to the compost pile. All the spent scapes of the daylilies can join the compost pile, as can their faded leaves. Cut back the iris and watsonia foliage.

Did you prepare a new bed for the divided daylilies? They need division every three or four years. Now is a good time to do so. Using a spading fork, dig the overgrown clump. Have your hose handy. Wash off the soil and you will see where to divide the clump. If it won't pull apart, use your knife. Cut back the leaves for easier handling.

The roses will need pruning next month, but get a head start by raking up and disposing of the fallen rose leaves. These bear any fungus or rust spores and you don't want them in your compost pile. A little prevention now will save spraying later. Do you have any climbing roses? Retie them to prevent wind damage later.

Check for wandering blackberry seedlings. When the ground is damp they can be pulled out easily. Just wear your heavy gloves. Pick up any fallen fruit. There may be enough raccoons in your neighborhood to prevent many windfalls, but the raccoons near me seem to prefer climbing trees.

Have snails been climbing the lemon tree? Secure a copper cuff at the bottom of the trunk. Local nurseries carry this product.

Have the gophers been tunneling in your garden? I know of no infallible deterrent, but have had some success with flashlight battery-powered buzzers. Gophers won't eat daffodils, so a daffodil "fence" can protect other bulbs they fancy. Favored plants can be planted in hardware cloth cages. These can be constructed using tin snips with hardware cloth from the hardware store. Do not buy chicken wire as the holes are too large. Fasten your cage with the wire that comes on a spool. There is a castor oil-based repellent available in nurseries that can be sprayed on the flower bed. I feel the winter rains may dilute its effectiveness. But it is worth a try. Another stratagem is garlic salt, applied into the gopher hole. Here, too, the rain may dilute, but may work if the hole is fresh. The smoke bombs sold for gophers are fairly useless, but highway flares burn longer and can work. Cover all holes with pieces of wood and leave one hole open. Light the flare, insert and have a hard-hearted helper waiting at the lower hole.

If you have hellebores in your winter garden, mulch them with a little gravel. It will protect the leaves from the unsightly black fungus.

Remove finished compost and give the roses and perennials a tonic. Add all your brown leaves and foliage to the top and add a sprinkle of blood meal to get the new pile started.

Don't forget your tools. Clean off mud and plunge them up and down in a pail of sand to which you have added a bottle of oil. Wipe wooden handles with boiled linseed oil. They will rest, free of rust until spring. Enjoy all the plant and seed catalogues you have waiting in the house.

Fall Checklist for Christmas Blooms

~

by Jane Scurich

I don't believe I have ever enjoyed so many glorious summer evenings outdoors, dining al fresco on our patio. Perhaps I have forgotten some of our last twenty-five summers here, but I must say, in my mind, this one has been splendid.

With all the fabulous warm weather, it is easy to forget the tasks necessary to fill our homes and gardens with beautiful blooms for the holidays and into the dreary winter months. So take a stroll and identify all last year's holiday plants, which have been summering in your garden. Chances are they have replenished themselves with new energy and are ready to create another big show. Here's what I found and what I'm doing to encourage rebloom.

Christmas Cactus

After a long season outdoors in the filtered shade of my tulip magnolia, I am going to withhold water from my Christmas cactus (*Schlumbergera*) for the month of October. If the rains start, I'll have to move them to a more secluded space. Flowering is related to day length and nighttime temperatures. Optimal temperature range is between 55° and 65°F for six weeks, which should happen in my California garden. If these temperatures are not possible for you, move the plants to an area of total darkness in October and remove them when buds form. Do not overwater and do not injure Christmas cacti at the soil line, as they are prone to be infected by root rot.

Amaryllis

I moved the amaryllis out of watering range, the pots are drying out and the long green foliage is withering. Cut off the foliage close to the bulb. This will force the bulb into dormancy. Place the potted bulb somewhere cool and dark—such as in your basement or a cabinet in the garage. Ideally the bulb should have total darkness for a period of ten to twelve weeks. Around January or February you can bring the bulb back out, remove the old soil and roots and repot. Begin watering again and in about six weeks you should have a bloom.

I have never been successful in bringing my amaryllis back into bloom for the Christmas holidays, but I love filling the house with these stately beauties in February and March. I buy new bulbs each fall to pot for holiday bloom and add to my collection. If you cannot plant the amaryllis bulbs immediately after receiving them, store them at a cool temperature between 40° and 50°F and be careful not to damage the roots.

As I was checking on the bulbs in my garden last week, preparing them for their required rest, I was thrilled to discover a two-foot flower stalk on one of them. Their blooms are as beautiful in September as they are in the winter!

Cyclamen

It's time to bring your cyclamen out of dormancy now. I leave mine in a state of semi-neglect after they complete their bloom cycle in late spring. Now is the time to give them fresh soil, an all-purpose fertilizer and water them thoroughly. Cyclamen are commonly attacked by mites that can be found around the buds. As the plant starts to grow, infested leaves become distorted, often curl inward, and foliage may become darker and appear streaked and blotchy. Mites can easily be brought home on infested plants from the nursery. Check plants thoroughly before buying, because these mites will spread to other plants! If I do find some, I will use a narrow-range horticultural oil called Mite X to bring them under control.

* * *

Wonderful bulbs arrive at local garden centers each fall, each bulb filled with new life, so pick up a few and plan your schedule to insure you have blooms to fill your house for the holidays.

Hyacinths

So easy to force! Just place the bulb in a hyacinth vase, add water to the base of the bulb and place the container in a cool dark place until it fills with roots. Then move the container to a cool bright spot and enjoy! Hyacinths usually flower in eight to twelve weeks.

Amaryllis

In addition to the re-blooming Amaryllis I mentioned above, I annually add a few to my collection. These spectacular blooms never go unnoticed. Select from a wide range of pinks, whites, reds and variegated colors. Either plant them in soil, leaving the top half of the bulb exposed, or grow them in an amaryllis vase with water, like the hyacinth. Place the pot in a warm, sunny room. Water sparingly until you see new growth, then water when the soil feels dry. Expect flowering six to eight weeks after planting.

Paper White Narcissus

One can never have too many of these fragrant charmers. "Force" them into bloom by placing large firm bulbs on a bed of pebbles in a container without drainage holes. Add water just to the base of the bulb and follow the directions given above for forcing hyacinths. Expect flowering about six weeks after planting. Starting in October, plant paper whites at two-week intervals to maintain a constant bloom supply.

While I am always a bit sad to watch the days grow shorter and acknowledge that my roses may be putting forth their last show of the year, I do look forward to opening my door to the intoxicating fragrance of the paper whites and knowing the holidays have arrived.

Clean Your House in the Spring, Clean Your Garden in the Fall

~

BY JEANNE PRICE

If spring is the traditional season to clean house, fall is the time to clean up your garden. Whether winters are severe or mild, this is when most plants rest before blooming in the spring and summer. So prepare your garden for a nap.

Trim spent flowers and stems on perennials. Cut off yellowing foliage and pull dead leaves from fountain-shaped perennials. Rake up fallen leaves, especially those that show evidence of disease like rust, thrips, black spot or mildew. This is especially important for rose leaves. The best disposal is to seal them in a plastic bag and deposit them in your garbage can. Do not put them in your compost pile or in your green can for pickup. These microorganisms will continue to thrive. Sealed in an airtight bag they will eventually suffocate at the dump.

If you can't get all the leaves up because they are mixed in with mulch, just cover with another layer of mulch. This will prevent the rain from spreading pathogenic fungi and prevent bacteria spores from splashing onto the plant this winter. Leaves also can shelter the eggs of slugs and snails. The brown garden snail (*Helix aspera*) and the gray garden slug (*Agriolimax reticulatus*) lay their eggs in October and November. As hermaphrodites, every snail and slug lays eggs.

Clean out the weeds still infesting your garden. If you have a compost heap, add your clean leaves to it. If weeds are coming up between pavers, pour boiling water on them. Much easier to do than to pull or pry them out and less toxic than herbicides!

Now is a good time to repair or put in a new lawn. Clean out the thatch and aerate the lawn before fall rains. Stake tall shrubs or young trees against the winter winds.

Always put your tools away clean, but if you've been lax, this is a good time to clean them. Pruners and loppers should be cleaned periodically during the year with denatured alcohol to prevent the transmission of diseases. Well-maintained tools are safer, too. Scrub down weeders, shovels, forks and trowels with steel wool soaked in vegetable oil. Sandpaper your tools' handles to prevent splinters in your fingers. To find your tools easily in the garden, paint the handles with fluorescent paint. Keep tools sharp by using a file on shovels and hoes and a whetstone on the blades of cutting tools.

Other autumn tasks include moving plants to let them settle into their new spots over the winter. Start a compost pile: place weeds in a black plastic bag, close it tightly and leave it in the sun for several weeks.

Autumn is harvest time for flowers as well as food. Hydrangeas make beautiful dried flowers. Now is the time to cut them as they are changing color. You can put them in two inches of water and let them dry, but I've put them in a vase without water and they dry very well. When you change to fresh bouquets, you can store the dried blooms loosely and they will serve you again.

My neighbor has an apple tree that overhangs my yard. At night I am startled at how explosive a ripe apple can sound as it hits the roof. This year the tree has produced a bumper crop. He doesn't use sprays of any kind and many of the apples are small, wormy or badly bruised as they fall on the gravel path. Some apples have been nibbled by small animals. Now and again I find one good enough to eat. If I don't put the inedible ones into my green can, I can liquefy them in my blender and pour the slurry around my plants and cover the mess with soil. Earthworms and microorganisms convert the slurry into nutrients for the plants. Other produce scraps from the kitchen only make the slurry better.

Find some inspiration in your garden and these chores will fly by. Ellen Sandbeck comments in her book *Eat More Dirt,* "Gardening is a wonderful way to learn through experience, annually. Millions of us thinking, pondering, meditating as we trundle about our dearly beloved gardens can be a dynamic and positive force in the world."

The Leaves Are Falling!

~

BY CHARLOTTE TORGOVITSKY

All across the country fall brings an abundance of leaves—a most familiar gift of nature. In a huge variety of sizes, shapes, textures and colors, they are nature's food factories. All life, including the earth itself, depends on their ability to convert sunlight, water and carbon dioxide into available nutrients.

During the summer, when there is plenty of sunshine and available water, the leaves of plants are busy photosynthesizing, literally "putting together with light." Plants, specifically the chlorophyll in the leaves of plants, use sunlight to turn water and carbon dioxide into glucose. Plants use glucose for energy and as a building block for growth; excess glucose is turned into starch and stored.

As summer days get shorter and the nights begin to cool, some plants are induced to stop chlorophyll production. Food has been stored for winter, and since sunlight is usually in shorter supply, this is a good time for the plant to rest or go dormant. As the chlorophyll in the leaves is reduced, the leaves are transformed into beautiful fall colors. The brilliant colors we associate with fall have been there all along. They are masked in spring and summer by the green color of the chlorophyll.

The orange colors are from carotene and the yellows from xanthophylls. Both are common pigments also found in flowers and foods like carrots and bananas. The reds and purples come from anthocyanin, the same pigment responsible for the color of beets, red apples and purple grapes. In some trees, like maples, glucose is trapped in the leaves after photosynthesis stops. The cool nights of autumn turn the glucose into beautiful reddish colors. Some trees, such as the deciduous oaks, drop an abundance of brown leaves in fall; the color is from waste products left in the leaves.

The biological mechanism at work in deciduous plants is called leaf senescence. At the base of each leaf is a special layer of cells called the abscission or separation layer. These cells facilitate the flow of water and nutrients to and from the leaf during the summer. As the daylight hours grow shorter, they begin to swell and form a cork-like material, reducing and finally cutting off the flow between the leaf and plant. At this point the leaves are just barely attached, and drop to the ground with the gentlest of autumn winds.

These dead leaves are valuable stuff in the bigger cycle of things. They settle onto the soil as a blanket, sheltering the plants and all sorts of life from the harshest of winter temperatures. Insects use the leaf litter as a sheltered place to overwinter. Many birds, such as the towhees, robins and thrushes will hunt for a meal in the leaf litter. Decomposers, such as earthworms and sow bugs, are busy earning their living and, in doing so, returning essential nutrients to the earth.

As organic gardeners, we can make the most of this autumn bounty. Leaves can be left where they fall to enrich the soil in a most natural manner. For finer mulch, leaves can be put through a shredder, and then applied to more formal garden beds.

Leaves can also be used as one of the layers in a sheet-mulching reclamation project. Areas not previously cultivated can be prepared in fall for spring planting. First, remove as much of the weedy growth as possible, then spread newspaper and corrugated cardboard over the area. All sorts of compost materials, including leaves, can be piled on top of the paper layer, to a depth of about a foot. Left over the winter, the thick paper layer smothers any unwanted weedy growth, and all the materials decompose to create a rich organic soil ready for new plant growth.

In our garden, we are creating habitat in the vicinity of a venerable old English oak, over one hundred and twenty-five years old. The tree is deciduous, and the bounty of leaves in fall is almost overwhelming. We leave a layer of leaves about six inches deep in our native shrub border. The rest are raked up to create leaf mold, which can be used the following year as a top dressing and to supplement other planting areas.

Leaf mold is easy to make: It is a form of passive composting that requires little attention once the bins are set up. We use a heavy-duty wire mesh to form a bin about four feet high and perhaps three feet in diameter. The bin can be secured to the ground with U-pins or earth staples. Leaves are then deposited in the bin in layers about seven or eight inches thick. Between each layer sprinkle blood meal; this accelerates the decomposition of the leaves, which are mainly carbon, by adding nitrogen. Water as you create the layers, and water occasionally during the dry months as well.

Our leaf mold bins were five feet deep in leaves last January. Now we have twelve inches of beautiful, deep brown, rich leaf mold to use as we continue planting out our habitat understory.

Winter Spraying with Dormant Oil

~

BY JANE SCURICH

*"Limited Time Opportunity—This offer may expire in thirty days
(depending on the weather)."*

We are often inundated with opportunities that expire in a few days—specials that offer to save us money if only we act now. This is a slightly different kind of opportunity—this offer allows you to be kind to our environment by using low-toxicity products to minimize your garden pest problems. But, as the advertising lingo goes, "You must act now."

The dormant season, that window of time when our fruit trees and roses lose their leaves and show no new buds, offers the ideal opportunity to eliminate overwintering insects and fungus by spraying the plants with a horticultural oil. Not allowing a new generation of insects to hatch will allow you to have a much more trouble-free garden and eliminate the need for pesticides.

Visit your local nursery for a selection of horticultural oils (often called dormant oils). These oils are highly-refined petroleum oils manufactured specifically to control pests on plants. Dormant oils work by suffocating the eggs or overwintering stages of insects. Scales, mealy bugs, aphids, leafhoppers, whiteflies, mites, and eggs of many species can be controlled with the proper application of horticultural oils. Oil is considered a "contact insecticide"—only the insects present at the time of application will be affected. Beneficial insects and our feathered friends who visit your plant later will not be affected.

Lime sulphur is often added to control many common diseases, overwintering fungal spores, mites and psylla. The addition of copper-containing compounds with a minimum of 50 percent copper is necessary for the control of peach leaf curl and shot hole, both diseases of stone fruit varieties.

The ideal spray day will be clear and windless with temperatures between 40° and 70°F. Temperatures remaining above 50°F for at least twenty-four hours after spraying will allow the oil to spread over the tree and into all the crevices. Spray early in the day to allow the plant to dry and do not spray if frost is predicted. Use a tank-type sprayer for best coverage, start at the top of the plant, and thoroughly cover all branches, twigs, and the trunk. Obviously, your ideal day might not manifest itself during the dormant season and you will need to select a day that most closely fits your needs.

Several very important rules of use will insure your safety and the well-being of neighboring plants and your hardscape. Using a less toxic product still mandates personal caution and responsibility.

- Always read and follow the manufacturer's directions.
- Mix only what you can use. You cannot save the prepared solution for later use.
- Shake, don't stir, oil-based products for complete blending.
- Dormant spray is meant for plants with no leaves. Don't attempt to control the scale on your citrus with a dormant spray. If your rose still has leaves, remove them. Your plant needs a rest and now is the time.
- Always wear a mask when spraying your plants. Wear protective clothing, long sleeves, a hat, chemical-resistant gloves, and anti-splash goggles.
- Wash your hands and face immediately after using these products.
- Dormant oil sprays may prove caustic to annuals growing under or nearby the object of your spray. Cover tender vegetation before spraying and don't remove until all residue has dripped off.
- Rake and remove all leaves and debris before you spray. Spray the soil around the base of your roses to control powdery mildew and black spot.

✦ The oil mixtures can permanently stain concrete, stucco, brick and other hard surfaces—cover them first with plastic or tarps.

A minimum investment of time and money can bring you much peace of mind in your garden this spring and summer. When you shop for the dormant oil, you will no doubt find the relatively new, superfine, ultra fine or supreme type oils that can be used year-round and are safe for citrus and other foliage. But for spraying your rose and fruit trees in the winter, look for dormant oil, follow the directions carefully, and enjoy a pest-free spring!

Embracing Winter as a Gardener

~

BY DARLA CARROLL

Gardening in winter is in some ways gardening at its very best. It is all about dreaming, planning, and wondering. What will your garden look like next year? Do you want to try a new color scheme? Maybe an all-white garden bed? What new projects will you plan? An arbor with *Clematis* 'Venosa Violacea' and *Rosa* 'Phyllis Bide'? What new plant or plants do you want to try to grow?

Perhaps I'll give that *Daphne odora* another try. Maybe I won't kill it this year. If I dig a hole as deep as the root ball (plant it high enough to have really great drainage) and at least twice as wide, amend it with compost and cover with mulch and water it just right, it could happen.

This is also the very best time for drooling over garden books and catalogs, with their alluring descriptions and glossy photographs offering seductive images of what our gardens could look like. Think about where you can possibly fit the most wonderful, floriferous, hardy, fragrant, disease-resistant, rare, new plant that no one else in your neighborhood is sure to have? I know I have room for one or maybe three!

A few of my favorite catalogs have just started coming in the mail. The one from White Flower Farm (www.whiteflowerfarm.com) always tempts me with its lush photos and delicious verbiage especially about its many varieties of daffodils. One year I bought their daylily and daffodil mixture and it has given me years of easy care pleasure. The catalog from Sheperd's Garden Seeds (www.sheperdseeds.com) always makes me want to plant a few seeds, even though I almost never get them planted at the right time. The catalog from Digging Dog Nursery (www.diggingdog.com) has no lush photographs, but it does have beautiful line drawings of the various plants and great information about each plant as well as creative ideas for planting companions.

This is the season when we don't have to think about the sweat and the back aches, we are not preoccupied with weeding or other chores, or the worry that we never have enough time to keep up with it all. Gardening in all its down-to-earth practicality can for now be a delightful dream. For now, in this dormant time, we can wander unhurried through our garden of the future, the garden of our mind—confident that everything will be much better this year.

Surely, this year will be the one where everything will grow and flower just like the glossy photographs in the catalogs. Lacking opportunities to directly experience being in the garden with its many smells, sounds and feelings that directly connect us to nature, we can be nourished by the storm of images flowing through our minds.

This wintertime garden dreaming provides an important opportunity, a necessary pause to recoup from our labors. Allowing a fallow time, in the world as well as in the garden, is a necessary part of cultivating individual creativity and personal expression in a world where opportunity for creativity and expression is increasingly limited.

In our 16-16-16 society (top growth is all), one is tempted to suppress or deny the need for 0-10-10 (strong roots). Sleep, dormancy, rest: these are ideas that are an often disregarded and disrespected part of a natural cycle that allows for strong roots to grow that will then allow new top growth to burst forth renewed and refreshed.

So this winter, give yourself and your garden that time to relax, to go dormant, to dream of the coming year. Give your plants some 0-10-10 and be prepared to burst out into new growth in the spring.

Care of Gift Plants

~

BY JANE SCURICH

'Tis the Season! December is the time for entertaining and lots of drop-in friends and relatives. The doorbell rings and guests arrive with the perfect hostess gift—a blooming plant, the pot gaily wrapped in shiny gift paper and a big bow. Chances are, this holiday present will be either a poinsettia, a cyclamen or a Christmas cactus. With a little tender loving care, you can encourage your gift to continue to brighten your home well into the New Year.

The typical winterized home can be a hostile environment to plants far from their native land. The poinsettia was introduced to the United States in 1825 by Joel Robert Poinsett, first U. S. Ambassador to Mexico, who gathered plants in the wilds of southern Mexico. The common name for this cherished symbol of the Christmas season came from his last name. Botanically, the plant is known as *Euphorbia pulcherrima*. The Christmas cactus, *Schlumbergera bridgesii*, is a South American native and a succulent, not a true cactus as the name implies. *Cyclamen* are a genus of plants containing twenty species, which are part of the family of Primulaceae, the primrose family. In the wild, cyclamen grow around the Mediterranean, being natives to parts of Europe, western Asia and parts of North Africa.

Coming from such geographically diverse cultures, what traits do our favorite holiday plants have in common? They do not like having their feet wet, they do not tolerate drafts from a fireplace or furnace vent and they do not like sitting on top of a television. Good drainage is essential to the longevity of these traditional holiday blooms. So, the shiny foil wrap must go! While the wrap makes the plant look more festive and protects the giver and the recipient from handling a damp and not terribly attractive plastic pot, it also inhibits air circulation and prevents water from draining. So thank your giver, place your colorful parcel on the buffet, and when the party is over, get rid of the foil wrap and find a place in your home which will best suit the needs of your new plant.

An easy way to accommodate your plant is to place the plastic pot into a larger cachepot, an ornamental container designed to hold flower pots. To release your creative energies, paint a few clay pots and saucers with acrylic paint and have them on hand to accommodate these seasonal delights.

Both the poinsettia and the Christmas cactus should be watered when the surface is dry to the touch. Water the soil until it runs freely out the drainage hole in the container. If a saucer is used, discard the water that collects in it. Do not leave the plant standing in water. Overly wet soil lacks sufficient air, which results in root injury. Plants exposed to high light and low humidity require more frequent watering.

These plants will enjoy a bright location, out of direct sunlight. A window that faces south, east or west is better than one facing north. To keep the poinsettia in bloom, maintain it at a temperature of 65 to 70 degrees Fahrenheit during the daylight hours and, if possible, move it to a cooler place at night. Root rot disease is more prevalent at temperatures below 60 degrees Fahrenheit so don't leave your poinsettia in a cold room. The cactus prefers a cooler temperature; a range from 65 during the day to 55 at night is ideal. *Cyclamen* prefer to be kept moist and can wilt quickly. Water at the soil level but keep moisture away from the area on the tuber where the leaf and flower stems grow. If that gets wet, the plant may rot. Make sure pots have drainage holes and don't allow water to accumulate in the saucer. *Cyclamen* prefer cool temperatures; daytime temperatures between 60 to 65 degrees Fahrenheit and night temperatures around 50 degrees Fahrenheit are ideal.

Most all of your houseplants will benefit from being watered in the morning with room temperature water. Enjoy your brightly colored holiday plants and keep them around through the dreary days of winter with just a little bit of thoughtful planning to meet their cultural needs. Happy Holidays!

Spring Soil Strategy

~

BY MELISSA GEBHARDT

Spring is a time of renewal and growth, synonymous with fertility. Gardeners themselves spring to action at the first sign winter is over and the yard is awakening, most armed with big bags of fertilizer and a hose-end sprayer. Yards are blindly assaulted with gallons of green (or blue) life-giving liquid known as fertilizer, or dry little pellets are scattered to the four winds. No plant is left uncoated, dripping the nutrients that will hopefully result in the best garden on the block. While the resulting riotous growth looks good, is this really the best for the plants, or for the birds and bees that rely on plants for food?

Synthetic or inorganic fertilizers and amendments (those that do not occur naturally but are manufactured) are a quick and inexpensive way to get visible results but may not be the best for the environment or the plants themselves as they leach into the water table and draw on resources to manufacture. Organic options, on the other hand, more slowly release nutrients and can be more expensive, but have the added benefit of improving soil structure and water infiltration—especially in tough clay soils.

STARTING AT GROUND LEVEL

There are at least seventeen nutrient elements that are essential for healthy plant growth. Carbon, hydrogen and oxygen are taken up by the plant primarily through the air and water. Nitrogen, phosphorus and potassium are the primary nutrients in inorganic fertilizers and are expressed in percentages: 10-10-10 means 10% of the total bag is nitrogen, 10% is phosphorus and 10% is potassium; the remainder is filler.

Nitrogen is the most "glamorous" and consequently overused of the nutrients, for it is responsible for the green and leafy growth.

179

Phosphorus is essential to root growth and promotes seed, flower and fruit formation. It is important in established gardens as well as when seeds are started. Potassium improves the size and quality of fruit and vegetables and increases resistance to disease. Other essential nutrients needed in minute amounts include calcium, magnesium, sulfur, iron, boron, and other trace minerals.

The availability and uptake of inorganic nutrients is largely dependent on soil pH—the measure of alkalinity or acidity, expressed on a 1-14 scale. Plants generally perform best in soil at a slightly acidic to neutral pH (6-7). Soils that are very acidic (pH less than 5) may have low levels of plant-available nitrogen, phosphorus, potassium and other micronutrients. Highly alkaline (pH greater than 9) soil can be lacking nitrogen, phosphorus, manganese, and iron and may also contain high concentrations of damaging salts. There are simple home tests available at local garden centers to determine soil pH. A more detailed analysis of pH and specific nutrient content can be performed by a professional laboratory.

SOIL MAKEOVER

With or without a pH test, a close look at the plants themselves will reveal what they need. For example, a lack of iron will show up as yellowing between the veins of citrus leaves and often happens in alkaline soils. Low nitrogen may result in yellowed leaves and slow growth.

All soil can benefit from the addition of compost, either homemade or purchased, as it provides all that the soil needs to be productive and also improves clay soil structure by loosening it up and allowing air and water to move more freely.

Animal manures (often mixed with decayed plant material), such as chicken or steer manure, are commonly used and supply a broad range of nutrients. Fresh manures (straight from the farm) need to be applied about a month prior to planting an area, or allowed to age before application. Fresh manure is too "hot" and will burn plants. It is generally thought that chicken manure is more potent than steer, horse or dairy manure. Well-rotted manure can be applied immediately. Both help condition the soil.

Manures or compost can also be made into a "tea" and poured into the garden—soak one cup of manure or compost per gallon of water for two to three days.

HOME RECIPES

Gardeners can also create their own concoctions of common and more exotic natural fertilizers. Quick nitrogen is provided by alfalfa meal, bat guano, blood meal, cottonseed meal, feather meal, fish meal, sea bird guano, and soybean meal. Phosphorus (if needed) can be provided by bat or sea bird guano, as well as bone meal and rock phosphate. Green sand, glacial rock dust, kelp meal, oyster shells, and sunflower hull ash can add potassium and trace elements. Some of these additives can be found in packages on garden center shelves, while rarer additives may be available by the pound. A no-cost option is to obtain coffee grounds from a local coffee shop to add nitrogen to compost or apply directly to acid-loving plants like rhododendrons, blueberries and azaleas. In addition, many farms and stables will provide fresh manure. Be aware that weed seeds may sprout.

NO SINGLE ANSWER

There is no standard solution for all gardens, and the needs of an individual garden will continually change and practices must be re-evaluated. Experiment with different mixes for different plants to find the right combinations for your garden. There are environmental considerations when deciding on fertilizers, but just as the nutrients in the garden need to be balanced, these considerations need to be balanced with financial limitations and personal preferences. Gardening provides a fresh new opportunity each spring to "branch out" and try something new, just as the garden does each year.

Tiptoe through More than Tulips Next Spring

~

BY MELISSA GEBHARDT

What could possibly give one so much with so little effort as planting bulbs? These non-descript brown blobs lumped into the category of bulbs includes true bulbs (like daffodils, tulips, lilies), corms (squatter in shape but similar to true bulbs), tubers (bigger, irregularly shaped with "eyes"), and rhizomes (spread horizontally).

What they all have in common is that each is a compact power-house of food and energy, easily buried in the ground which results in a burst of flowers months later. Sometimes you may forget you even planted them, or exactly where, until the foliage pops up after long winter rains and a spectacular flower emerges. Everyone is familiar with and has probably purchased tulips and daffodils, but tulips need pre-cooling in order to produce flowers and typically do not come back the next year unless they are in a cold climate. There are many other impressive bulbs, often under-utilized, that can increase our garden palettes.

Spring-blooming bulbs are a great reward for sitting through the months of rain or snow. *Hyacinthoides hispanica* (wood hyacinth) has blue, pink and light blue flowers which multiply over the years and look great in a woodland setting with ferns, along with *Dicentra's* (bleeding heart) dangling white or hot-pink hearts with ferny foliage. *Anemone blanda* (Grecian windflower) has cute daisy-like flowers and perks up part-shade areas and *Scilla* (spring squill) look nice along paths with their blue/purple flowers and will also multiply. *Allium karataviense* is a unique bulb from the onion family sporting five-inch white spheres of little flowers above foliage with red edges.

An all-time favorite are the lilies, and one can grow florist-quality flowers with little effort and have them blooming from June into September. The selection of *Lilium* is quite extensive and available for both fall planting and early winter planting. Asiatic lilies provide pops of bright orange, yellow, pink and red in early and mid-summer. These lilies are available with and without spots, stripes, and some even have interesting "recurved" (curved backwards) petals. Tigrinum (tiger) lilies are tall and floriferous (twelve to twenty flowers per stem), with maroon spotting. The oriental lilies, such as popular 'Star Gazer' and 'Casablanca,' perfume the air in mid to late summer and are beautiful in white, pinks, and maroons. Chinese trumpet lilies are yet another group of lilies, with a graceful shape and provide large blooms in late summer.

There are other sizzling summer blooming bulbs, that really jazz up the garden. Dahlias have become more popular, and range in shape from tight pom-poms to twelve-inch "dinner-plate" size on five-foot-tall plants. I was given *Watsonia* corms a few years ago, and did not know they would grow into a 3- to 4-foot-tall plant, with sword-shaped leaves and lovely sprays of hot-pink flowers. In a different part of the garden, *Crocosmia* 'Lucifer' rewards me with sprays of flowers, this time red. I have been able to divide both of these over the years and pass them on to friends and family.

Spring bulbs can be ordered via catalogue now, or will be in garden stores in the fall; summer bloomers available after the first of the year. I typically plant at or after Thanksgiving weekend, so that they do not come up too early and get the benefit of our winter rains. Plant in very well drained soil and be sure to follow directions on planting depth. "Plant six inches below surface" means six inches above the top of the bulb and is a minimum depth.

Fertilize and spread bait for snails when growth first appears, and always allow the foliage to die back to yellow or brown before removing bulbs, so that they will bloom again the next year. In addition, limit water in the area once the bulb has finished its bloom to discourage rot. You will be rewarded again and again.

CHAPTER SEVEN

Garden Design

The Evolution of a Family Garden

~

BY ANITA JONES

When designing a garden you are lucky if you get to start with a clean slate. Our Novato home was six years old when we moved in and although the slate wasn't completely clean—we had mostly lawn, a few trees and some insignificant perennials—it was a relief not to have large areas of unwanted plants to rip out.

As first time homeowners, having never grown much beyond the obligatory potted philodendron years ago in college, ficus and ferns in apartments along the way, and roses in pots on the deck of the San Rafael townhouse we rented before buying, my husband and I were both novice gardeners. We were eager to lay brand new shovels to our very own soil.

In October, we moved in and began work in earnest the following March. My husband produced an aerial view map of the property to scale showing the footprint of the house and existing trees and shrubs. We used copies of this to experiment with various layouts. I signed up for Master Gardener training.

Our daughter was three years old when we moved in, so we needed a family garden—something for everyone with room to grow. Our goals included a play area with some lawn, herb and vegetable beds, flower beds, a child's garden, shade, nooks for sitting and entertaining and a site saved for the future garden shed.

We focused our attention first on the rectangular, south facing back garden, simultaneously designing the play area, adjacent beds and the child's garden. The site for one of the beds came with a dramatic backdrop: a row of five redwood trees that stand in our neighbor's yard lining the forty year-old grape stake fence we share. A priority in the back yard was shade. Most often we based our choice of trees on advice from people with garden conditions similar to ours who had thriving trees we liked. Among our choices are eastern red-bud, crepe myrtle, Chinese scholar tree, Santa Rosa plum and red leaf Japanese maple. My husband built an arbor in the southwest corner and we planted a different vine at each post. The first summer—as we awaited the promised shade—I painted a large canvas with designs echoing those of the lawn furniture and this formed a fine shade canopy.

The play area called for removing a fifteen by twenty-five foot area of sod and replacing it with sand and a large redwood play structure. We relocated the sod to the front yard where we'd planned a large berm. Had we known then what we know now, we would never have done this. For cosmetic reasons the previous owner tilled the weeds and laid new sod over them. The weed seeds lay in wait beneath our new berm. Seven years later we are still fighting the transplanted weeds and sod.

In the north facing front garden, along the entire length of the split rail fence we share with our neighbor, a misguided honeysuckle vine had been forced to grow as a hedge. This was our biggest challenge months later when we decided to remove all of it, showcasing the handsome fence.

For vegetables and cutting flowers in the narrow east garden, we built three triangular raised beds. The morning sun makes this the ideal place for our potting bench.

The west garden, also narrow, we call the living room. Here we planted an oval rose garden defined by an Idaho quartz path that leads through the gate to the front and in the other direction to the arbor. Redwood Adirondack chairs sit in a corner well-shaded now by the maturing Japanese maple. During the month of May the living room is transformed for our annual May Festival. We plant the may-pole in the center of the rose garden and for a month the garden is alive with music and dancing children as they rehearse and perform traditional dances.

Planting was a backbreaking task. Every hole had to be carved out of the hardpan clay that covers the property and the soil amended. Over the years, my husband has dug down deep enough to hit the dark, loamy soil that reminds us that this land was once a walnut orchard.

To complete our goals, three years ago my husband built the 8-by 12-foot shed. More of an artist studio, it houses a potters' wheel, sink with running water, shelves and a workbench. Like families, gardens are ever-changing, reflecting our whims and filling our needs. So much work has gone into the making of our garden, sometimes we have to remind ourselves to sit in the shade and let the garden give back to us.

Treehouses: Not Just for Kids Anymore!

~

BY MARIE NARLOCK

If your family is graced with children and your backyard is graced with a majestic oak or a small grove of towering redwoods, then perhaps there is a treehouse in your future. In fact, even if children aren't in your equation, then an adult treehouse might be a unique, tranquil addition to your yard.

Let's start with what defines a treehouse.

When I was little, a wedged-in slice of discarded plywood provided a 12-foot-high lookout roost from my grandmother's maple tree. When I sat on that small platform it was just me and the blue jays in our own private nest. From my throne in the sky I was the self-proclaimed "Queen of the Backyard," literally and figuratively above it all. Despite its obvious lack of OSHA-approved building methods, it provided hours of pleasure and (amazingly) no injuries ever occurred.

Would I let my own children play on that precarious perch? It's hard to say. Fast forward thirty years and the treehouse in our own backyard today has a railing and is partially screened in to avoid possible falls.

One of our family's projects for this summer is to enlarge this treehouse. "Easy," I thought. "We'll just make it a little taller and wider and call it a day." Somewhere along the line I obtained a copy of *The Treehouse Book* by Peter and Judy Nelson and David Larkin.

That book changed everything.

Suddenly my definition of a treehouse expanded exponentially. There are treehouses with plumbing, electrical, claw foot bathtubs, leaded windows, and fireplaces, some with full kitchens, some with architectural features to die for. There are cozy treehouse bedrooms, practical treehouse home offices, and inviting treehouse guest houses.

190

Some have simple, old-fashioned approaches, and some have spiral staircases and rope bridges. There are some low to the ground and some suspended eighty feet in the air, specially designed to rock in the wind.

Apparently, the only thing standing between my grandmother's perch and a small home high in the trees is imagination. Oh, and time, money, and know-how. Those, too.

Suffice it to say that we will be making our treehouse "a little taller and wider." However, I'm sure that a few of the details of the enticing examples in the book may find their way into our expanded creation.

For those considering a building project up in a canopy, I highly recommend this book as well as the website www.thetreehouse-guide.com.

As for the basics, keep in mind the following:

- Choose the right tree and have an arborist check it out before embarking on your project. As a general rule, trees with hard wood (oak and maple) are good choices provided the tree is free of pests and diseases. Buckeyes, aspens, poplars, and alders are less desirable choices. Trees with U-shaped branch junctions tend to work better than those with V-shaped junctions.

- Do no harm. Don't cut the bark and the cambium layer any more than is absolutely necessary. Cutting too deeply may risk killing the tree or a major branch.

- If you aren't a licensed contractor, consider joining forces with one. True, there are all sorts of do-it-yourself guides out there. There are even treehouse plans that can be purchased with the novice in mind. Let your own experience level be your guide. It may sound outrageously expensive to hire a contractor, but the payoff may be great. Who knows? With today's frothy real estate prices, your quaint little project may ultimately add up to valuable square footage!

- Find out about any zoning laws, such as setback requirements, if you think there might be a problem. You may think that a cute little cottage in the sky for your kids looks friendly; your neighbors may think otherwise.

- Location, location, location. If you have a choice, be sure to select the tree with the best view, easy access, and a bit off the beaten path. The pleasure you will derive gazing up at your children in their sweet little fort will all be lost if you're constantly having to worry about their accidentally dropping items on your head. You don't want to have to warn visitors of possible air strikes either. Don't make your treehouse understory a hard-hat zone!

If this all seems too overwhelming, take heart: there are public vacation treehouse resorts available all over the world, just waiting for you to visit. It's the closest possible thing to a Swiss Family Robinson vacation. And one thing is guaranteed: you're sure to have a great view.

Designing a Garden For Children

~

BY SALLY LUCAS

When I'm invited to discuss a design for a new garden, it's always exciting to discover if children are part of the family and will be sharing the outdoor space. Before I get home to my drawing board I'm already imagining how to incorporate a skate park, four-story tree house, sand pit, climbing frame, racetrack, totem pole and soccer field into the forty-foot-by-twenty-foot space! Of course, the reality is that if the garden were dedicated entirely to the children's needs, I would be back three years later to re-design when their interests had changed.

So when it comes to designing a play area for children, most adults would look through catalogues of playground equipment and select what they think would be appropriate for their children. This is pretty easy and doesn't take a lot of effort. However, is this really what children want?

Outdoor spaces designed by children would, I believe, include plants, water, flowers, dirt, sand, mud, birds, insects, places to sit in, on, under, and lean against. They would provide shelter and shade, but also would be full of opportunities for adventure and play. If children could design their own gardens they would be places where children would want to stay all day.

Start by making a wish list of how you want to use the garden and include all the family's ideas in the discussion—even the most outrageous. When it comes to creating a garden to match your family's personalities and style, you are the expert in knowing what you want. Then, compromise! Perhaps an alternative to the four-story tree house is a play tent, which can be used as a hideaway—remember that scale is negotiable.

These are practical landscape considerations to consider in your plan:

* Choose a style that suits you and your home (e.g., formal, wildlife, English, Mediterranean).
* Consider placing the play area where you can see it from the rooms you spend most time in.
* Children will need safe surfaces that are comfortable for bare feet and not slippery when wet.
* Create a place for family gatherings or a place for kids' outdoor lunches.
* Make paths wide enough for two people to walk down.
* Protect utilities such as pipes, lighting, cables and septic systems.
* Make the garden adaptable to the children as they grow.

When you have reached agreement on what to include in the garden, take time to draw up an accurate plan of the site including existing features such as buildings, trees and features you wish to retain. Make several photocopies and try different variations on the plan. First add paths and then add any structures you have agreed upon. Keep it simple, but include all your best ideas. Annotate the plan with any important notes such as the sunniest corner, a good view, a slope or an eyesore you wish to disguise.

The last, and for me the most exciting and creative part of garden design, is the planting. Select plants that complement the style of garden you have chosen, but avoid spiky plants such as *Phormium* or plants with thorns like *Berberis* that could harm small children. A small number of plants are toxic and could make your child ill if eaten, for example, *Brugmansia* and *Ligustrum*. Some plants such as the *Euphorbia* species cause a skin irritation on contact and are toxic when ingested. Read plant labels carefully and if in doubt check with garden center staff or call your local Master Gardener desk.

When I was a child I asked my father for a small patch of land where I could grow my own plants. My father was a vegetable man and he had no time for flowers. On the one occasion my mother planted a *Camellia* bush, it was replaced the next week with cabbage plants as my father did not recognize it and therefore considered it a weed! My early garden trials included lettuce, peas and radishes, all of which are quick and easy to grow during the cool season.

My last word on gardens for children concerns the use of water. I will not take the risk of placing a permanent water feature in a garden where children play. However, provided constant surveillance is provided, a simple paddling pool or hosepipe will provide hours of fun.

Gardening with a Japanese Touch

~

BY JULIE MONSON

In May, I visited Kyoto and toured ten of its fabulous villa and temple gardens. My favorite garden this trip, however, was in a Kyoto suburb, and belonged to the Nakamuras, our hosts for the week. Theirs is a private, quite small, domestic garden that can be viewed from the four main rooms of the first floor. My favorite memory of our visit was sitting on the tatami mat at the edge of the "tea serving" room in the early evening, my feet on the steppingstone leading into the garden, watching the pine, moss, shrubs, and water basin slowly darken in the dusk. What, I wondered, are the lessons that could be learned from this simple, carefully designed, small garden? Here are some of the garden elements that can be incorporated into American home gardens.

The Nakamuras' totally enclosed garden is about fifteen feet wide and forty-five feet long, with three planted focal points, each landscaped with plants and a few carefully chosen rocks. Steppingstones lead from one end to the other, past a simple four-foot open bamboo fence, which serves to define the more important "tea ceremony" area. To walk from one end of the garden to the other is to take a journey.

ENCLOSURE

The Japanese have devised ingenious ways to surround their homes, entryways and gardens with walls, hedges and fences to provide privacy, and also to provide a backdrop that judiciously defines outdoor space. In my host's garden, the garden wall had been covered with cedar bark. In front of this is planted a twenty-five-foot tall evergreen hedge that creates the effect of a dark forest. This is pruned yearly and I was lucky enough one morning to watch the gardener climb up into this "forest" and remove enough foliage to permit light and air to enter the garden.

SCALE

Because a small garden like the Nakamuras' recreates an idealized nature, every tree, rock, shrub and fern is scaled to fit the space. Small-leaved shrubs and the one pine are regularly pruned to show their trunk and branch structure and to limit their growth. Carefully sited rocks are grouped under the plantings and a stone lantern and water basin are in scale with the other elements of the garden.

SIMPLICITY

Japanese gardens are quiet, serene green spaces with few flowering shrubs, perhaps azaleas, nandina, a miniature plum, and iris by a water source. The variety of plant material is limited and most likely evergreen. Open empty space is as important as space filled with shrubs and ferns. "Less is more" is the rule. Simple rock and gravel pathways and drainage areas duplicate the contours found in nature.

METICULOUS MAINTENANCE

The Nakamuras' garden requires two kinds of maintenance: a professional gardener who comes twice a year to prune everything and perhaps add or remove a plant, and the daily cleanup of removing fallen leaves and debris and refreshing the water basin. This garden is sprinkled daily in summer to keep the moss fresh and to cool down both house and garden.

A VIEWING PLACE

Small gardens like this are meant to be seen from a special vantage point. In the house, each of the downstairs rooms has sliding glass doors that can be opened to the garden. The small Japanese garden must be designed with the viewer in mind. Homeowners can use a picture window, deck or patio as their special viewing place.

Excellent References

Visit Japanese gardens in your area to gather ideas. Published resources include: *A Japanese Touch for your Garden* (Seike/Kudo, Kodansha International Ltd., 1985) and *Enhance Your Garden with Japanese Plants* (Glattstein, Kodansha International, 1996).

Enhancing Wealth through
Water Structures

~

by Terumi Leinow

Would you like to enhance wealth, prosperity and have an abundant flow of opportunities in all areas of your life? Then consider including water structures in your garden or patio. According to Chinese principles of Feng Shui, water is symbolic of wealth, and the appropriate placement of water structures can help enhance wealth.

The words Feng Shui means "wind" (*feng*) and "water" (*shui*). Feng Shui is about vital life force—*chi*. Feng Shui weaves together the elements of wood, fire, earth, metal and water to achieve balance and harmony. Gardeners work intimately with each of these elements and as a result, are naturally aware of this life force called *chi*. Gardeners also are attuned to the importance of water; the garden gives instant feedback when it gets too much or not enough water.

Asian gardens always include a water feature such as a fish pond, cascading stream or water fountain. This is because water is such a powerful metaphor; water is indeed the source of life for every living thing on our planet. In Feng Shui water has many meanings and associations. Water symbolizes abundance, wealth, prosperity, wisdom, career, business, social life and cash flow! Therefore choosing and placing water structures in the garden can help activate many of these qualities. Wealth, of course, relates not only to money, but also to wealth of family, friends, health, creativity and more.

There are three important factors to consider when placing water structures in the garden: location, size and shape of the structure, and movement and quality of the water. The ideal location for a water structure is in either of two primary areas of the property or garden. One is referred to as the wealth area. As you enter the property, the area in the far left is considered the wealth corner. Featuring a water-fall, pond, or water fountain is ideal in this location. You can also place a water fountain on the patio or deck on the wealth corner of the house. This area is located in the left corner relative to the front door.

The second beneficial area to place a water structure, especially bubbly water fountains, is in the garden by or near the front door. The front door is considered the "mouth of *chi*" for it is here that opportunities for wealth and success enter the home.

When considering types of water structures, one could include a cascading waterfall or stream in the wealth corner. It is important that the flow of water be directed towards and not away from the house. A pond or water fountain in this location is also suitable to stimulate prosperity and wealth. Ponds attract wildlife and beneficial insects that further contribute to vitality in this area. Ensure that the size of the water structure is in proportion to the house—not one that overpowers. Ponds that are round, oval, or kidney shape and embracing, i.e., curved towards the house, are ideal.

Be sure that there is a circulating pump in the pond or water fountain; stagnant water is to be avoided! If you wish to include fish in the pond, the Japanese carp is considered auspicious. Also popular are nine goldfish (eight gold and one black). Fish symbolize wealth and success and bring movement to the water.

Ensure that water fountains, especially ones placed near the front door are uplifting and bubbly rather than drippy or sputtering! Remember that the purpose of all these water structures is to stimulate and activate the flow of wealth. It is also important that the sound of the water be soothing and pleasing.

Wealth springs from an inner source of well-being. To sit in the garden surrounded by nature's beauty, exquisite colors, and to hear the sound of water, can only fill us with deep gratitude, peace and profound joy.

Dogs: Delightful or Devious in the Garden

~

BY DIANE LYNCH

Alice, my little mellow mutt, is my constant companion in the garden. She's rarely more than three or four feet away, snoozing, as she waits for me to move somewhere else so she can follow. Recently she decided that the nice soft bed of yarrow looked inviting, so it's looking a little rumpled these days, but that's about the extent of the damage she inflicts. Her other personality emerges at the farm where she spends hours digging and stalking gophers. Fortunately she rarely damages plants in the mature orchard. Dogs can be a great pleasure or a real nuisance in the garden, depending on temperament and circumstances.

Dogs who dig can create havoc in a nice garden as they uproot plants and destroy turf. Dogs are pack animals and need companionship. Sometimes boredom is the culprit when families are gone long hours and Fluffy is home alone with nothing to do. Leaving the dog in the house or having someone come in to play with him or walk him are possible solutions. Local Humane Societies offer Behavior and Training Classes as well as behavior consultations and private training to address specific issues. Obedience training will certainly help to prevent some problems and is a good idea for all dogs.

If your dog is digging for gophers, try getting rid of them. You can try one or more of the many suggestions I've tested and discarded: stuff plastic bags in burrows, bury fish heads (but many dogs find these very attractive), dump in powdered garlic, cayenne pepper, dog droppings, Juicy Fruit gum, kitty litter, etc. Or try the battery-operated noisemakers or castor oil repellant sold in hardware stores. The only success I've had is trapping the critters and planting new plants in chicken wire cages. As for getting the dog to stop digging for gophers, try the repellants.

One fellow built a sandbox for his dogs so they would have a digging spot of their own and found that they loved it, resolving the problem instantly. If you opt for this, try to locate the box so it gets both sun and shade and make the sand at least two feet deep. Bury rawhide bones and toys for the dog to find.

Some diggers especially like newly seeded lawns and fresh plantings. Laying chicken wire on a new lawn will foil their efforts and using a tomato cage or ring of chicken wire around a new plant will give it some time to root in and not be so tempting. Sometimes the best way to deal with an energetic, digging dog is to divide the yard in half, either with a fence or an "invisible" barrier. On one side have a nice garden for you and on the other sturdy grass (bermuda grass or other running grass with rhizomes or stolons will hold up best) or decomposed granite for doggy. Lawns, besides being the most labor and water consuming use of land, aren't always great for dogs because their urine and droppings can kill patches.

Some dogs aren't diggers but their energetic running and habitual patterns will create paths—go with the flow here and put stepping stones, mulch or decomposed granite down and make them look intentional. There are plenty of rugged plants that will hold up to all but the most destructive dog. Some that come to mind are:

- Thorny roses such as rugosas aren't very nice to brush up against and they make beautiful red "hips" in the fall and require little care or pruning.
- *Dietes* or fortnight lily have stiff upright leaves and flower all summer.
- Ivy, which is toxic to dogs, and *Vinca*, which is on the noxious weed list, will hide droppings and stand up to some dog traffic although they're also great habitat for rats and mice.
- *Liriope* looks like tall grass and produces purple flower stalks in August.
- *Phormium*, New Zealand flax, comes in a wonderful array of colors and sizes and has stiff upright leaves.

Sometimes neighboring dogs are a problem when they invade un-fenced areas or their owners look the other way as they deposit their little (or large) piles in the petunias you've so lovingly planted and tended. Try offering the wayward owner a plastic bag (I always have a folded newspaper bag in my pocket) to clean up after Fido. Berberis or barberry, which comes in shades of green and several reds, is a spiny-stemmed shrub that can be effective in keeping dogs out of gardens and provides a nice looking informal border.

Bonemeal and dried blood are instant magnets for dogs, who think you've planted a juicy steak just for them. Look for amendments that have other ingredients such as alfalfa pellets or cottonseed meal or use chemical fertilizers in moderation. There are several repellants on the market but they must be re-applied frequently and are very unpleasant smelling, both to dogs and humans. Be very careful which pesticides you use as many are toxic to dogs. Rat poisons can contain warfarin, which will cause internal bleeding, and should always be placed out of reach of dogs and children. Keep dogs off turf for twenty-four hours after applying chemicals such as herbicides and pre-emergents. Slug pellets containing metaldehyde are tasty as well as poisonous to dogs; try nighttime missions with a flashlight to round up these pesky diners. Sluggo contains iron phosphate and the label states that it is safe for pets.

Dogs can be joyful companions in the garden, but their needs and instincts must be taken into account when designing a garden. Figuring out what is going on with the dog, and remedying the situation, such as providing companionship or stimulation in cases of boredom, often solves problems. By observing their habits and needs we can creates spaces that will be beautiful and beneficial to us and allow our canine friends to be a viable part of our gardens also. My garden would be a lonely place without my buddy Alice and her mother Milly, who's so old she sleeps in the sun most of the day.

Gardens Can Keep Memories Alive

~

BY ANITA JONES

Four years ago my daughter and her friends were swinging and play-ing in our Novato garden, as I clunked around in knee-high rubber boots working in a nearby flowerbed. The squeak-squeak of the swing sent me to the garage for that handy can of oil spray. It also sent my head spinning into a dejá vu: I saw myself forty years before swinging on the rusty swing set of my Georgia childhood, my father clunking around in knee-high boots working in his garden. The squeak-squeak of my swing sent him to fetch the can of thick, dark grease used for this purpose.

Seven years ago I knelt between our white Adirondack chairs planting a stand of gladiolus bulbs (*Gladiolus grandiflora*) when I was interrupted by an important phone call relaying sad news, the death of a friend who had breast cancer. Each year when those yellow glad-ioli bloom they flood me with memories of my friend—playing vol-leyball, raising her daughter—before she fell ill.

Fifteen years ago in the garden of our home in Albany, Georgia, my late mother planted a bed with vibrant pink phlox (*Phlox maculata* 'Alpha'). Every year since, they've come back strong. In memory of her I planted the same variety in our California garden.

Gardens help us keep memories alive. Sometimes it happens quite serendipitously—as with my squeaking swing story— but we don't have to wait for dejá vu. We can approach the garden with full inten-tions of making it a living vessel for memories. We can use the garden to blow the trumpet and beat the drum for past and present events and loved ones. Here are four ways to design your garden with mem-ories in mind:

ART PIECES

In our garden we have two patinaed relics of days gone by. One is a bronze Adidas tennis shoe—a wonderful gate-stop—and the other is a bronze Viking helmet, both artifacts from my husband's college days. Unfortunately things went terribly wrong during the pouring of his bronze Viking bust and the helmet is all that survived. It makes for colorful storytelling with visitors to our garden. Nestled in a bed of day lilies we have a ceramic casserole, hand-thrown by my husband. Open the lid and reveal sand and shells from our honeymoon seventeen years ago in Kauai. Doubling as a piece of playful art, this weather-proof exhibition case keeps the contents clean and dry waiting to reward whoever is curious (or nostalgic) enough to take a peek at our tropical souvenirs.

PLANTS

The stand of yellow gladioli and the bright pink phlox harbor fond memories of my friend and my mother. A flowering cherry tree (*Prunus*) we planted in memory of my late sister is a beautiful tribute to her in the early spring when in full bloom. However, my husband's longing to have the scent of common lilac (*Syringa vulgaris*) from his Wisconsin childhood will never be realized in our northern California garden. Our winters are too warm. Therein also lies a caution: don't allow your romantic notions of certain plants blur your ecological responsibility. Before planting, check to be sure you are not choosing an invasive non-native that should not be planted in your climate zone.

GARDEN FURNITURE, TOOLS AND PROPS

A weathered 1960s lawn chair from the porch of my family home and my late father's antique garden tools make this is an area where whimsy meets memento in our garden. A favorite prop, which is only brought out during special occasions in the garden, is my refurbished childhood Schwinn, circa 1964.

HARDSCAPE

Paths in the garden guide visitors to destinations you have chosen. You can put emphasis on the journey by incorporating items that hold memories and tell stories: stepping stones made by your children as they grow, boulders and stones of various sizes inscribed with quotes and quips from family members or others, bricks or architectural elements rescued from the demolition of a house or building that holds special memories for your family.

As with so many aspects of the garden, when it comes to creating a space for restrospection, you are limited only by your own imagination. So with ecological caution and nostalgic whimsy, go forth and enjoy turning your garden into a living keepsake.

APPENDIX:
Demystifying Botanical Names

~

By Julia Flynn Stiler

I caught the gardening bug years ago from Nancy Julian Siler, my mother-in-law. The author of numerous books, two of which have been optioned by Hollywood, Nancy is also a long-time member and former board member of the Garden Club of America, as well as a knowledgeable horticulturalist. She's the reason I've visited so many astonishing gardens in Britain and the United States.

Before I left from our last visit with Nancy at her home in Tennessee, she quietly tucked a slim, yellow brochure into a packet of other materials she'd gathered for me to take home. It was entitled "Do You Speak Latin?" and has a quirky line drawing of a Greek fellow, dressed in a toga, orating on a pedestal, on the front.

Nancy wrote this pamphlet for the Garden Club more than two decades ago and it's the clearest explanation I've yet read for why we struggle with Latin names for the plants in our gardens. I'm shamelessly borrowing from her brochure (with her permission) in hopes that other gardeners find it as helpful as I have.

WHY USE LATIN?

It was only natural that as soon as man identified a certain plant, he gave it a name. Unfortunately in early times, the same plant was being given a dozen different names in a dozen different parts of the world.

To avoid mass confusion the seventeenth and eighteenth-century herbalists (who laid the foundation of modern botany) named all the plants in Latin. Educated Europeans at this time were still speaking and writing Latin in their studies. Today accepted names for all plants are Latin names or names made into Latin forms.

WHO STARTED THIS?

If you know only two kinds of roses, white and red, it is easy to name them Rosa alba and Rosa rubra. However, when you need to identify twelve different kinds of white roses, as Carl Linnaeus did in 1753, the problem compounds.

To distinguish between two white roses Linnaeus wrote: "Rosa caule aculeato pedunculis laevibus, calycibus semipinnatis glabris" and "Rosa caule petiolisque aculeatis, calycis foliolis indivisis." Hopeless for our purpose.

Then Linnaeus hit upon the happy device of using a single word following the name of the genus to indicate the species. This one word, usually an adjective, describes one feature of the plant, sometimes not an especially important feature; but since the adjective is used only once in that genus, it identifies one, and only one, plant.

This binomial (two-name) system is indispensible today to botanists and gardeners the world over who are interested in accurate identification.

IT'S EASIER THAN YOU THINK!

You already know more Latin botanical names than you realize. These Latin names (and dozens of others) have become common forms: Crocus, Cyclamen, Delphinium, Gardenia, Hibiscus, Hydrangea, Iris, and Narcissus are a few. The Latin name is no harder to learn if you start with it. Pronunciation need not be a problem.

To quote L.H. Bailey, "There is no standard agreement on rules for pronunciation of botanical binomials." You may go for the Latin pronunciation, or you may simply pronounce generic and descriptive names as if the words were English.

As for the accent: in words of two syllables the accent is usually on the first. In words of several syllables the accent is usually on the next to last syllable. Exceptions abound.

The next step is to tackle the groupings. Let's start with family names.

~Appendix ~

FAMILY

Genera which are more or less alike and probably related by descent from a common (though distant) ancestor are placed together in one family.

The name of the family is usually formed by adding "–aceae" to the name of one of its genera. Examples of several families with representative members include: Liliaceae—Asparagus, Hyacinthus, Tulipa; Asteraceae—Ageratum, Aster, Chrysanthemum, Zinnia; and Iridaceae—Crocus, Freesia, Iris.

GENUS

Within a given family are plants with different characteristics separated in a general way—what we now call genera.

When our eighteenth-century herbalists came across a group that wasn't named, they often made up a name using a Latin stem. Botanists did not name plants after themselves (not considered good form!), but were often most generous in naming genera after friends or famous people. Examples include:

- Dieffenbachia—named in honor of Dr. J. F. Dieffenbach, in charge of the Royal Palace Gardens in Vienna.
- Begonia—named for Michel Begon, Governor of French Canada and patron of botany.
- Blighia—tropical tree named for Captain William Clark of Lewis and Clark fame.
- Bougainvillea—named for Louis Antoine de Bougainville.

Most families have a dozen or more genera. The Orchidaceae family has over 600 genera. The Ginkgoaceae family has only one genus, the Ginkgo.

Genus and species are the most useful plant names to know. They are the binomial (two name) system.

Species

Within each genus are many kinds of plants different in specific ways—the species. Each distinct type is identified by a single word (not capitalized) immediately following the genus. Examples (first general—then specific) and (first genus—then species) include: *Cornus florida*, *Crocus minimus*, *Magnolia grandiflora*, *Trillium catesbaei*.

The descriptive word is usually an adjective Latinized to match the genus in gender. Thus the confusion of -albus, -alba, -album depending on whether the word it modifies is masculine, feminine or neuter. All three mean "white form" and only vary to conform to the gender of the genus word.

A few examples of this: -japonica means from Japan. But to match the gender of the genus, it is modified as *Humulus japonicus*, *Fatsia japonica*, and *Acer japonicum*. Likewise, -alpinus means from the high mountains. It is modified as such: *Aster alpinus*, *Anemone alpina*, and *Papaver alpinum*.

The identifying species word may be (instead of an adjective) a person's name or an indication of geography—usually Latinized to conform. Thus, catesbaei (honoring Mark Catesby), fraseri (named for John Fraser), gallicus (from France) and exoticus (from a foreign country.)

Variety

Within the species are still smaller units, the most common being variety. This is indicated by a third word, usually written: *Primula sinensis* var. *fimbriata* or *Cornus florida* var. *rubra*. Another division is form and can be written *Cornus florida* F. *rubra*.

Yet another division is cultivar, an acronym meaning "cultivated variety." This is correctly written in single quotation marks: *Anemone blanda* 'Radar' or *Aquilegia hybrida* 'Snow Queen.'

An indication of the parentage of the hybrid is shown with an x, which literally means "cross with." Examples include *Camellia hybrida* 'Cornish Snow' *C. cuspidata* x *C. salvuensis*.

Hybrid and patented roses are known for promotion purposes by un-Latin names, such as Peace, White Masterpiece, and Blaze.

These within-the-species divisions and subdivisions can be almost as confusing as pre-Linnaean days. Just remember that variety is a subdivision of species, and there are several ways to indicate variety.

Thank you to Nancy Julian Siler, my mother-in-law, who wrote this guide to botanical names for the Garden Club of America.

Author Biographies

~

Maggie Agro is an illustrator and writer whose garden is just another creative medium in which to dabble. A mosaic of tiny plants with bits of shimmering glass, a pebbled ghost image of a meandering stream, a patchwork of plants that thrive and those that don't—her garden exhibits both loving care and benign neglect—a reflection of the happily imperfect human who tends it.

William Bentley was born and was raised in Watsonville, California. After spending thirty-three years as a tax and business specialist, he retired in 1992 to pursue a career in sculpture and photography and to continue his interest in home gardening. In 1994, he started the Master Gardener course offered by the University Of California Cooperative Extension. He did not complete the course in 1994 due to a severe accident. In 2001, he completed the course and has been active ever since. He has written articles for the *Marin Independent Journal*, completed several community projects and is currently working on a creek renovation project at The Redwoods in Mill Valley, California. He currently has an extensive home garden that has been included on several garden tours.

Darla Carroll did not develop a passion for gardening until she was an adult and moved to San Anselmo, California. She recalls as a child planting carrot seeds with her brother. To her amazement, the seeds sprouted. Without water, the tiny plants soon died. As a teenager, the idea of gardening in the cold, damp summers in San Francisco made no sense to her. However, when she became a homeowner, she decided to learn at least a little about gardening. The more she learned, the more she enjoyed gardening. She became a Master Gardener in 1998 and her love for gardening has continued to deepen over the years.

JULIE WARD CARTER, a lifetime volunteer of Marin Master Gardeners, served as President in 2000-2001 and as an Integrated Pest Management coordinator. Presently, Julie conducts seminars on Integrated Pest Management in Northern and Southern California. Julie also has a Residential Care Facility for the Elderly and continues her emphasis on less-toxic gardening in working with the residents on five-acre Creek Haven Gardens in Auburn, California. She practices as a dental hygienist in Calistoga, CA, and resides in Auburn with her husband, three cats and a dog.

ELIZABETH NAVAS FINLEY is a Master Gardener who was inspired by her training to become a garden designer after two decades spent writing on landscaping for newspapers and magazines.

VIRGINIA HAVEL is a longtime home gardener in Inverness. She is a retired biology teacher at the College of Marin, a founder of the Environmental Forum of Marin, and an active member of the California Native Plant Society. Her special interests are gardening with native plants and controlling exotic pest plants in natural landscapes. She writes a regular gardening column for the *Point Reyes Light* newspaper.

MELISSA GEBHARDT became a Marin Master Gardener in 2000, after living in her Mill Valley home for five years battling deer, fog and the hillside the house is perched upon. Six years later, three children have arrived and she has used her Master Gardener knowledge to create a garden that accommodates the family and her love of plants. Melissa now has four small gardens on our hillside—two are fenced in from the deer and two are open to the deer. The fenced gardens include a vegetable patch and a "secret" garden of flowering plants with a playhouse. The unfenced gardens are deer-resistant and range from a lush full-shade garden to a sunny xeriscape garden open to the Marin hills. Melissa teaches garden classes at her children's schools and writes a garden column for a mother's club newsletter, as well as articles for various publications.

ANITA JONES is a native of Albany, Georgia where she grew up close to the southwest Georgian land of red clay, pine trees, and pecans. Her father, a lardrenderer by trade, was a backyard farmer who raised bird dogs and chickens and grew vegetables for the table. Her mother was a teacher and librarian who loved growing flowers. Anita's passion for "all things garden" is anchored in those roots. A visual artist, writer and storyteller, she incorporates the three in workshops and residencies for children and adults. She spent over twenty years working as a fashion model and actress before turning her attention full time to homeschooling. A Bay Area resident since 1985, Anita received certification as a Marin Master Gardener in 1999. She lives in Novato, California with her husband and daughter.

TERUMI LEINOW is a certified Feng Shui and Space Clearing Consultant who draws on multiple traditions to restore harmony and balance on both inner and outer levels. She completed a three-year master's training program inspired by Grand Master Lin Yun, the world's leading authority on Black Sect Tantric Buddhism Feng Shui, and was certified as an Environmental and Personal Clearing Practitioner by Eric Dowsett, a pioneer in this field. Terumi also has more than thirty-five years of multi-national business experience. Additionally, she is a third degree karate black belt and founded the first All Women's Karate School in Canada. She became a U.S. resident with her marriage in 1994 and recently co-authored *Tuning In: Simple Rituals for Everyday Living.* She co-chairs the Marin Master Gardeners' Integrated Pest Management committee.

SALLY LUCAS was first introduced to gardening by her father, who allowed her to have her own vegetable plot. He also taught her that one cannot expect to take goodness out of the soil without putting it back. This was demonstrated each fall with the delivery of a huge pile of cow manure that required backbreaking task to dig it in. Much later, when she became the owner of a two-acre plot on a windy Scottish hillside, she realized she really didn't know where to start. That was the beginning of her passion for good, practical design. After gaining a diploma in garden design, Sally began a business helping home-owners transform their gardens. Moving to California tested Sally's ability to transfer her skills to a new climate and culture. To her surprise, she realized there really wasn't that much difference in the plant material and good design is, well, good design.

DIANE LYNCH has been a Master Gardener since 1996 and currently writes a garden column for her local Tiburon newspaper, *The Ark*. A long time organic gardener, she tends an ornamental/habitat garden in Tiburon and a mixed orchard and vegetable garden in Freestone in her spare time.

KATIE MARTIN has a Master's degree in Botany from San Francisco State University. Her love of running and the outdoors led to the publication of *Hiking Marin, 141 Great Hikes in Marin County* with her husband. She is the editor of the Master Gardeners' weekly gardening column in the local newspaper. Katie likes to use California native plants throughout her garden for their qualities of deer resistance, easy maintenance and low water use.

JULIE MONSON gardens on the Inverness Ridge in West Marin, California, a shady, cool environment suitable for Japanese maples, azaleas, and mossy ground covers inside her deer-protected court-yard. Outside the courtyard, she experiments with deer and fire-resistant native shrubs and perennials. Julie also volunteers in the small garden around the Inverness Library, a Master Gardener project, and has worked on numerous garden improvements there. For many years, Julie has had a strong interest in both gardening and in the history of landscape architecture. She enjoys her Master Gardener association, and is a member of The Garden Conservancy and the California Native Plant Society.

MARIE NARLOCK is a happy mom and gardener in Corte Madera, California, who feels lucky beyond belief to live in such a gorgeous spot on the earth. She volunteers for a handful of horticultural causes including her kids' school gardens and various Master Gardener projects. Marie enjoys growing edibles and is also learning about the joys of habitat gardening. She has studied landscape design and horticultural therapy at the University of California Berkeley Extension and Merritt College in Oakland and holds a B.S. in Journalism.

LEE OLIPHANT gardens year-round in the coastal village of Cambria, California. Her garden produces vegetables, fruits, and berries that thrive in the mild, temperate climate. Influenced by a visit to Monet's garden in Giverney, France, Lee has transformed her garden into a bouquet of color with flowering plants such as roses, Irises, geraniums, Cannas and poppies. Exposed areas are filled with the more muted drought-tolerant, deer-resistant varieties of lavender, sage, and erigeron. Lee, a retired educator, Ed. D., received her Master Gardener training in Marin County and is presently an active member of the San Luis Obispo chapter of Master Gardeners. Lee writes for professional education publications and is the garden columnist for *The Cambrian*.

ELIZABETH R. PATTERSON gardens and lives with her family in Ross, California. She grew up in Michigan where long, cold winters and the renewal of spring fostered her love of nature. She studied biology in college and received a Masters in Public Health on the east coast and then moved west to California. She has spent the last nineteen years in the Bay Area adjusting to the Mediterranean climate, putting down roots and practicing the art of nurturing on her spouse, children, pets and garden.

JEANNE PRICE has lived in Belvedere, California for almost fifty years. Currently she lives in a cottage with what she describes as a California-cottage garden—the look of a cottage garden with Mediterranean plants. The gardens in her life have ranged from two acres to zero and she believes the best is the one she has now. It gives her pleasure visually and provides hands-on experience. It is not too large to work in effectively, nor too small for privacy. It incorporates both pots of flowers and large trees. She is a relatively new Master

Gardener (2003) and is constantly learning about plants, plans and pests while trying to practice what she learns in her own garden and in the community. She learns much from other Master Gardeners and wishes that your gardens thrive and give you joy.

JANE SCURICH grew up in Memphis, Tennessee, where her Dad owned a large "feed and seed" store. She loved to accompany her Dad to work or to visit the numerous "truck farmers" who supplied Memphis with fresh produce. Her Dad grew sweet corn, luscious tomatoes, and Kentucky Wonder beans, along with enormous, fragrant peonies and his favorite rose, 'Peace.' Jane shared his passion for growing things, but with one significant difference: The first modern insecticide "DDT" came to market in the 1950s and her Dad, as others, believed it was the answer to all evils in the garden. Current knowledge shows us the dangers of the overuse of pesticides. Jane encourages others to learn the benefits of Integrated Pest Management techniques and lower the use of pesticides in home gardens.

JULIA FLYNN SILER is a business journalist who moonlights as a garden writer. She discovered her love of gardening while living in England as a foreign correspondent for Business Week magazine and then for the Wall Street Journal. One of her most memorable visits was to Sissinghurst Castle and its famous "white garden," developed by Vita Sackville-West. She later visited many other famous gardens in Britain, often accompanied by her mother-in-law, Nancy Julian Siler, an avid gardener and garden writer who lives in east Tennessee. She has put aside her own gardening efforts, for the moment, while she finishes a book on the Mondavi wine empire, tentatively titled *House of Mondavi*, which will be published by an imprint of Penguin USA in 2007.

ANNIE SPIEGELMAN is a Marin Master Gardener who was raised and hardened on pavement in New York City. She is the author of *Annie's Garden Journal: Some thoughts on Roses, Life, Weeds and Men* and *Growing Seasons: Half-baked Garden Tips, Cheap Advice on Marriage and Questionable Theories on Motherhood.* "The Dirt Diva," a.k.a. Annie Spiegelman, is the garden columnist for *The Pacific Sun* newspaper. *The Dirt Diva's Almanac*, a book of garden essays, will be in bookstores next year.

CHARLOTTE TORGOVITSKY's interest in gardening began at a young age, when her family immigrated to California. As a Dane, born in Bombay, India, she had never lived in a place where she felt she really belonged. That changed when her Dad gave her her own little garden plot. She considers the land she lives on her only home and is happiest when she can share it with lots of native creatures. She is engaged in a course of study on the Natural History of California, and takes great pleasure in spending time outside, in the garden, hiking, and camping. Charlotte is Garden Education Manager and Volunteer Coordinator at the Marin Art and Garden Center in Ross, California. She manages a small nursery at the Center, allowing her to collect seeds and propagate to her heart's content.

MARYROSE WHELAN has spent a long life gardening in Virginia, Wisconsin, Davis, California, and finally in Mill Valley. The transition from the valley to coastal California was dramatic, but so was the change from Virginia to the northern plains. It all contributed to a gardener's education and made the adventure interesting. Roses have always been a favorite, especially antique varieties. While she was living in Wisconsin in the 1950s, a professor named Jake Boiser alerted Maryrose to the danger of oversudsing detergents to the water supply. Thus began her concern for water conservation. Sharing discoveries, plant cuttings and divisions with friends are some of her greatest pleasures.

Index

~

A. ameloprasum 98
A. sativum 98
Abelia 30, 158
Acer palmatum 76
African iris 150
agapanthus 17
agastache 161
alfalfa meal 181
alfalfa pellets 136
allium 17, 106
Allium karataviense 182
Allium sativum 98
almond shells 131
Alstroemeria 63
Alstroemeria pelegrina 64
amaryllis 163, 165
amend 31
American Bamboo Society 68
American Bird Conservancy 25
Anemone blanda 182
Angelica 106
ants 143, 144, 146
aphids 36, 70, 95, 115, 147, 172
apical dominance 156
apple 17, 167
apple tree 83
apricot 17
Aquilegia formosa 10
arbor 188
Arbutus unedo 32
Arctostaphylos 11
Argentine ant 146
Armeria maritima 32
Armillaria root rot 115
army worms 108

arsenic 127
artichokes 82, 93
arugula 93, 135
Arundinaria 68
Asian gardens 199
asparagus 82, 93, 107
asparagus fern 149
Asparagus officinalis 107
aster 17, 135
autumn sage 32, 61
azaleas 130, 151, 161, 197

B. m. riviereorum 69
B. ventricosa 69
baby blue-eyes 23
Bacillus thuringiensis 115, 128
bamboo 30, 68
bamboo mite 70
Bambusa 69
Bambusa multiplex 69
Bambusa oldhamii 69
barberry 150
bark 39
bark chips 129
basil 82, 95, 97
bat guano 181
beans 81, 93
bee 12, 15, 49, 73
bee balm 106
beetles 36
beets 89, 93
bellflower 17
beneficial insects 3
Berberis 194
Berkeley sedge 45

Bermuda grass 139
berries 81
bindweed 139
bird feeders 7
bird habitat 24
birdbath 7
birds 3, 117, 119, 121, 170
black bamboo 69
blackberries 83, 161
black sage 62
black spot 35
bleeding heart 182
blood meal 136, 181
blue gama 45
blue-eyed grass 23
bluegrass 138
bluebells 31
blueberries 81
bone meal 86, 98, 127, 203
borage 105
bougainvillea 158
boxwood 30
brine curing 112
broccoli 93
broom 139
brown rot 115
Brugmansia 194
buckwheat 7
Buddha's Belly bamboo 69
Buddleia 6, 33, 157
bugs 128
bulbs 31, 45, 182
bull thistle 139
bulrush 46
bumblebee 16
bush anemone 157
bushtits 22
butterflies 3, 15, 18, 32, 49, 52
butterflies-in-the-wind 33
butterfly bush 6, 33, 157, 158

C. dolichostachya 'Kaga Nishidi,' 45
C. morrowii 45
C. griseus horizontalis 52
C. hearstiorum 53
C. thyrsiflorus 53
C. tumulicola 45
cabbage 93
cactus 65
calendula 4, 105
California fuschia 32
California meadow sedge 45
California pipevine 19
California poppy 6, 23, 71, 150
calla lily 150
Camellia japonica 30
Camellia sasanqua 30
Campsis 158
Carex pansa 45
Carpenteria 158
caterpillars 33
carnations 106
carrot 93
catmint 17
cattail 45, 46
cauliflower 93
ceanothus 6, 17, 22, 31, 54
Ceanothus arboreus 52
celery 93
chard 93
chemicals 6
chemical fertilizer 203
cherry tree 205
chervil 82
chi 199
chickadees 22
chicken wire 201
children 193
Chimonobambusa 68
Chinese Goddess bamboo 69
Chinese herbal medicine 120

Chinese scholar tree 188
chives 82, 95, 96, 106
Choysia 30
Christmas cactus 67, 163, 177
Chusquea 69
cilantro 95
citrus 114
citrus trees 83, 114, 116
clarkias 23
clematis 33, 161, 175
Cleveland's sage 62
Clivia 30
clover 24
cocoa bean hulls 130
coffee grounds 181
coffeeberry 6
columbine 7, 10, 17, 23
compost 3, 5, 21, 39, 42, 82, 180
composting 171
compost pile 167
container plants 40
copper 127
coral bells 10, 31
corn 93
Cortaderia 46
cosmos 6, 17, 32
cotoneaster 6, 31, 150
cotoneaster cover crop 127
cottonseed meal 127, 181
coyote 119
crabgrass 138, 140
creeping sage 62
crepe myrtle 188
Crocosmia 31
Crocosmia crocosmiiflora 32
culinary herb 60
cured olives 110
currant 6, 9
cuttings 67
cutworms 108, 115

cyclamen 164, 177
Cymbidium 74
Cyperus 45
Cyperus alternifolius 46

Dactylis glomerata 45
daffodil 162, 182
dahlias 183
dandelion 106, 139
Daphne odora 175
dates 120
daylily 161
deadheading 6
deer 49, 119, 149
deer mouse 153
deer-resistant landscaping 149
design 29
dianthus 161
diatomaceous earth 4
Dicentra 182
Dietes 53, 202
dill 19, 95
Diospyros 117
Diospyros kaki 118
dogs 201
dogwood 30
dormant oil 172, 173
drip system 4, 33, 39
drought 38, 41
drought-tolerant 120
drought-tolerant plants 32
drying 102
drying herbs 96

earthworms 130, 167, 170
eastern redbud 188
Echium 151
edible flowers 104
Eisenia foetida 132
elderberry 6
Eleagnus 30

elephant garlic 98
English lavender 72
English oak 170
Epilobium 32
epiphyllum 65
epiphytic cacti 65
Equisetum 45
Equisetum hyemale 33, 46
erosion control 53, 58
Escar-Go 130
Eschscholzia californica 6
Euonymus 30
Euphorbia 194
Euphorbia pulcherrima 177
Eureka lemon 116

family 209
Fargesia 69
fava beans 135
feather meal 181
Feng Shui 199
fennel 19, 97, 106
ferns, 30
fertilizer 82, 125, 136, 179
fertilizing 31, 34
fescue 45
fiddleneck 24
fig tree 33, 83
Figwort 19
filaree 24
finches 22
firebird penstemon 11
fish 200
fish emulsion 99, 127
fish meal 127, 181
flax 30, 45, 202
flowering quince 31
forget-me-nots 55, 106
fortnight lily 150
fountain 200
fountain grass 45

foxglove 17
freezing 102
French lavender 73
fruit 117
fruit fly 111
fruit tree 83
fuchsia 11, 21, 158
fungicides 34, 35
fungal disease 115
fungus 35, 130, 172

gall moth 53
Galvezia speciosa 11
garden design 187, 193
garden design for children 193
garden furniture 205
Garden Valley Ranch Nursery 34
garlic 98, 106
gaura 33, 161
genus 209
geranium 17, 30, 32
girasols 82
glacial rock dust 181
gladiolus 204
Gladiolus grandiflora 204
glue traps 155
gophers 70, 119, 162, 201
gooseberry 7
grafting 67
grapefruits 114, 116
grasses 30, 44, 135
Grecian windflower 182
green sand 181
grevillea 150
Grevillea 'Canberra' 11
ground cover 30, 33, 55, 61
groundsel 138
gummosis 115

habitat garden 3, 18, 22, 52
hard wood 191

harvest 101
hay 130
hazelnut 24
heavenly bamboo 151, 157
Hebe 30
hedge 30
hellebores 162
hemlock 19
herbal medicine 120
herbs 49, 82, 95, 102
herbicides 127, 142, 203
heuchera 23, 30
hollyhocks 32, 33
honeybee 12
honeysuckle 158
horsetail 33, 45
horticultural oil 36, 115, 172
house mouse 153
hummingbird 9, 15, 21, 32, 52
hummingbird fern 11
hummingbird sage 62
hyacinth 165
Hyacinthoides hispanica 182
hydrangea 157, 167
Hymenoptera 12

impatiens 21
Impatiens balfouri 23
Impatiens glandulifera 23
Indian paintbrush 19
Indian warrior 19
insecticidal oil 128
insecticidal soap 128
insecticides 6, 18, 36
insects 128, 144, 172
Integrated Pest Management 16, 35, 143
iochroma 21
irrigate 39, 42
irrigation 140
irrigation system 39
iris 161, 197

Irish and Scotch moss 57
iron phosphate 130
ivy, 202

Japanese garden 196
Japanese maple 76, 188
Japanese mustard 90
jasmine 158
Jerusalem artichokes 82
Johnny-jump-ups 106
jujube tree 120
Juncus 45
juniper 149

kinglets 22
Kniphofia uvaria 11
kumquats 114
kale 135
Kefir lime 147
kelp meal 181
Ketch-All 155

L. angustifolia 72
L. dentata 73
L. intermedia 73
lace bug 53
lambs ears 33
lambs quarters 138
Lamiastrum 30
Lamium 30
landscaping 41
lantana 158
Latin botanical names 208
Lavandula 32
Lavatera 157
lavender 32, 106, 161
Lavendula stoechas 71
lawn 29, 39, 140, 167
lead 127
leaf mold 171
leaf senescence 170
leafhoppers 172

leek 98, 106
lemon balm 82
lemon thyme 97
lemon 114
lettuce 89, 93, 135
lichen 57, 58
Ligustrum 194
Lilium 183
lily 53, 63, 182
lily turf 30
lime 114
limequat 116
lime sulphur 172
Linnaeus, Carl 64, 208
Liriope 30, 202
live oak 24
liverwort 57
logan berry 83
Lonicera 158
lotus 24
low-water garden 32
lupine 23
Lycopersicon esculentum 85

madrone 6
mallow 17, 138
manure 42, 127, 180
mandarin 114
manzanita 6, 11, 33
maple 6, 76
marigold 4, 104
marion berry 83
marjoram 82
Maxicrop 99
meadow mouse 153
mealybugs 75, 115, 147, 172
medicinal herb 60
mercury 127
Mexican bush sage 32, 61
Mexican mock orange 30
Mexican sage 10

Meyer lemon 84, 116
mice 152
Mimulus 7
Mimulus aurantiacus 11, 22
miniature plum 197
mint 82, 95, 150
Miscanthus 46
Miscanthus sinensis 46
mites 115, 164, 172
mizuna 90
mock orange 158
mold 52, 115, 130
Monarda 106
mondo grass 29
monkey flower 7, 11
monoculture 41
montbretia 32
moss 57
moss campion 57
moss pink 57
moth orchids 74
mulch 4, 31, 33, 39, 42, 58, 129, 141
mullein 139
mushrooms 115
Myosotis 55
Myosotis scorpioides 56
Myosotis sylvatica 55

Nandina 30, 151, 157, 197
narcissus 165
nasturtium 104
native plants 6, 18
navel orange 116
Neem oil 36
nepeta 72
newspaper mulch 130
nitrogen 179
Norway rat 153
nutsedge 139
nutshells 130

oak 6, 151
olallie berry 83
Olea europaea 111
oleander 151, 157
olive fruit fly 111
olive tree 110
olives 4, 110
onion 90, 93
opossum 119
oranges 114
orchid cacti 65
orchids 74
oregano 29, 82
organic gardening 125
ornamental grasses 44
Otatea 69
Oxalis 139
oxtongue 139
oyster shell 4, 181
oyster shell scale 53

pampas grass 46
paper white narcissus 165
parsley 19, 135, 81, 96
parsnip 93
passive composting 135
paths 206
peach leaf curl 173
peach tree 83
peas 81, 93
peat 58
Pelargonium graveolens 32
Pennisetum 46
penstemon 7, 17, 21, 32
Penstemon gloxinioides 11
periwinkle 25
peppergrass 90
Perovskia 158
persimmon 117
persimmon tree 83
pesticides 34, 127

Peruvian lily 63
Phalaenopsis 74
Philadelphus 158
Phlox 57, 205
Phlox maculata 204
Phormium 45, 194, 202
phosphate rock 127
phosphorus 179
Phytophthora 52, 142
Phyllostachys 68
Phyllostachys nigra 69
Pieris 158
pigweed 138
pine 6, 151
pineapple scented sage 22
pine needles 130, 161
Pittosporum 30
plum 17
plum tree 83
Podocarpus 151
Point Reyes Bird Observatory
    Conservation Science 24
poinsettia 177
poison oak 139
Policeman's Helmet 23
pollinating insects 5
pollinator 15
pond 200
Poor Man's Orchid 23
potassium 179
potato vine 33, 158
pot marigold 105
powdery mildew 35
predators 7
Pride of Madeira 151
primrose 104
propagate 50, 69
propagation 67
prune 35, 77
pruning 71, 81
Prunus 205

psylla 172
pumpkin 91
Pythium fungi 142

quail 24
Queen Anne's lace 19

R. officinalis 49
radish 88, 93
raised bed 4, 81, 100, 188
raspberries 81
rat 119, 152
Rat Zapper 155
red-hot poker plant 11
red wigglers 132
redmaids 23
redwood 29
reindeer moss 57
repellants 203
Rhamnus californica 6
rhododendron 130, 151, 161
rhubarb 82
Ribes sanguineum 9
rock garden 45
rock phosphate 181
Rodale, J. I. 126
rodenticides 155
roof rat 153
Rootone 67
Rosa 175
rose 32, 34, 106, 130, 158, 202
rosebush 34
rosehips 104
Rosmarinus officinalis 49
rosemary 33, 49, 72, 82, 95, 150
rugosas 202
rushes 45
Russian sage 158
Rust 35
Rutaceae 114

S. clevelandii 62

S. greggii 32, 61
S. leucantha 61
S. mellifera 62
S. officinalis 60
S. sonomensis 61, 62
S. spathacea 62
S. uliginosa 61
sage 7, 60, 82, 97
Sagina 57
salamander 31
salt curing 112
salvia 7, 10, 21, 60, 158
Salvia elegans 22
Salvia leucantha 32
Salvia splendens 60
San Francisco Epiphyllum Society 65
Santa Rosa plum 188
sanicle 19
santolina 72, 150
sawdust 39
scale 74, 115, 147, 172
Schlumbergera 67, 163
Schlumbergera bridgesii 177
Scilla 182
Scirpus cernuus 46
sea bird guano 181
sea pink 32
sedges 45
sedum 32, 135
Sevin 36
Shasta daisies 32, 33, 161
sheet composting 3, 135
sheet mulching 170
shepherd's purse 139
shot hole 173
shredded bark 141
shredded cedar 130
shrubs 30, 156
Silene 57
slug pellets 203
Sluggo 130, 203

slugs 4, 115, 130, 131, 166
snails 4, 115, 130, 131, 162, 166
snapdragon 11
snow-in-the-summer 33
snowberry 24
society garlic 33
soil 38
soil amendments 42
soil erosion 68
soil fertility 126
soil pH 180
Solanum 158
Spanish lavender 71
Spanish moss 57
sow bugs 170
soybean meal 136, 181
Spanish lavender 150
sparrows 22
species 210
sphagnum 58
spider 22, 144
spinach 135
spider mites 36
spinach 89, 93
spotted spurge 138
spring squill 182
sprouts 90
squash flowers 91, 93
squirrels 119
Stachys 33
star jasmine 30, 31
Steiner, Rudolph 126
sticky monkey flower 19, 22
straw 130
strawberry 4, 81, 150
strawberry leaves 104
strawberry tree 6, 32
striped orchard grass 45
sunflower hull ash 181
sweet alyssum 4
sweet marjoram 82, 97

sword fern 31, 53
Syringa vulgaris 205
syrphid flies 36

tangerines 114
Tanglefoot 147
tarragon 82, 96
thrips 36
thyme 82, 95, 97
toad 31
tomatoes 81, 85, 93, 103
toxic bait 155
toxic plants 194
toyon 6, 151
traps 155
tree mallow 157, 158
treehouse 190
trellis 83
trumpet vine 158
tulips 182
turnip 90, 93
Tyfon 90
Typha 45
Typha augustifolia 46

umbrella plant 46

variety 210
vegetable garden 81, 88
vegetables 101
verbena 72
vermicomposting 5, 132
Viburnum 31, 157
Vinca 202
Vinca major 25
Vinca minor 150
vines 156
violet 104
vole 153

water 199
water conservation 38
water retention 58

water structures 199
water well 86
waterfall 200
watsonia 31, 161
weed control 139
weeds 138, 166
weeping maple 76
western redbud 6
whiteflies 115, 172
wild rose 24
wildflowers 23, 45
willows 24
windbreak 68
wood chips 42
wood hyacinth 182
wood sorrel 139
woodland strawberries 150

woodpeckers 25
wooly thyme 150
worm bin 133
worm castings 132
worm composting 132

xeriscape 41

yarrow 17, 32, 72, 135
yellow jacket 12
yerba buena 33
yew 151

Zauschneria californica 11, 32
Zebra grass 46
Ziziphus jujuba 120
zonal planting 41
zoning laws 191

About the Editor

~

Barbara J. Euser is a Master Gardener who savors mornings in her hillside garden. She balances gardening and writing with a deep interest in international matters. She is a former political officer with the Foreign Service of the U.S. Department of State. As a director of the International Community Development Foundation, she has worked on projects in Bosnia, Somaliland, Zimbabwe, India, and Nepal. Her articles and essays have appeared in magazines and anthologies. She is the author of *Children of Dolpo, Somaliland,* and *Take 'Em Along: Sharing the Wilderness with Your Children,* co-author of *A Climber's Climber: On the Trail with Carl Blaurock* and *Heading and Distance Charts for the Colorado Fourteeners.* She is editor of *Bay Area Gardening.* In 2005, she directed writing workshops in the south of France and edited *Floating Through France: Life Between Locks on the Canal du Midi.* She lives near San Francisco with her husband. They have two grown daughters.